Elementary Poetry
Textbook and Activity Book

by Sonja Glumich

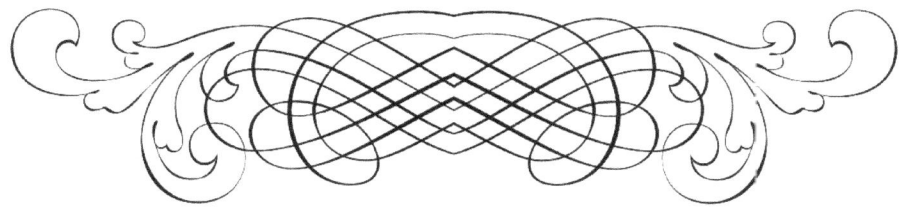

Poetry Study for Elementary School-Aged Children

Volume 5: Literary Devices

Interweaves poetry, recitation, narration, copywork, dictation, writing, and artwork

Under the Home Press Division
www.underthehome.org

Front Cover
Wooded Path in Autumn
Painting by H.A. Brendekilde (1902)
License: The author died in 1942, so this work is in the public domain in its country of origin and other countries and areas where the copyright term is the author's life plus 75 years or fewer. This work is in the public domain in the United States because it was published (or registered with the U.S. Copyright Office) before January 1, 1925.
original source: commons.wikimedia.org/wiki/File:H._A._Brendekilde_-_A_wooded_path_in_autumn_(1902).jpg

Copyright © 2020 Sonja Glumich
All rights reserved.

No part of this work may be reproduced, scanned, or electronically transmitted without prior permission of the copyright owner unless actions are expressly permitted by federal law the family exception detailed below.

The copyright owner grants an exception for photocopying or scanning and printing pages for use within an immediate family or homeschool co-op only. Scanned pages should never be used for any other purpose including sharing between families, posting online, transmitting electronically, or resale.

This exception does not extend to schools, however a reasonable licensing fee for reproduction can be negotiated by contacting Under the Home, the publisher.

For more information or to report errata, please contact Under the Home at contact@underthehome.org.

ISBN-13: 978-1948783057

DEDICATION

For Chris, Everett, Cassidy, and Calista – my beloved family and curricula test squad.

TABLE OF CONTENTS

PART I. RHYMING 1
    Lesson 1. "Remember" by Christina Rossetti 2
    Lesson 2. "All Things Bright and Beautiful" by Cecil Frances Alexander 6
    Lesson 3. "Christmas Carol" by Paul Laurence Dunbar 10
    Lesson 4. "Merry Autumn" by Paul Laurence Dunbar 14

PART II. ALLITERATION 18
    Lesson 5. "The Butter Betty Bought" by Carolyn Wells 19
    Lesson 6. "The Siege of Belgrade" by Alaric Alexander Watts 23
    Lesson 7. "The Eagle" by Alfred Lord Tennyson 27
    Lesson 8. "Pied Beauty" by Gerard Manley Hopkins 31

PART III. SIMILE 35
    Lesson 9. "A Visit from St. Nicholas" by Clement Clarke Moore 36
    Lesson 10. "A Lady" by Amy Lowell 46
    Lesson 11 "I Wandered Lonely as a Cloud" by William Wordsworth 50
    Lesson 12. "Birches" by Robert Frost 54

PART IV. METAPHOR 59
    Lesson 13. "The Sun Rising" by John Donne 60
    Lesson 14. "Shall I Compare Thee?" by William Shakespeare 65
    Lesson 15. "When I Have Fears" by John Keats 69
    Lesson 16. "Sympathy" by Paul Laurence Dunbar 73

PART V. PERSONIFICATION 77
    Lesson 17. "Stopping by Woods on a Snowy Evening" by Robert Frost 78
    Lesson 18. "She Sweeps with Many-Colored Brooms" by Emily Dickinson 82
    Lesson 19. "Mowing" by Robert Frost 86
    Lesson 20. "The Railway Train" by Emily Dickinson 90

PART VI. FORESHADOWING 94
    Lesson 21. "Spring Rain" by Sara Teasdale 95
    Lesson 22. "I Have a Rendezvous with Death" by Alan Seeger 99
    Lesson 23. "The Twins" by Henry Sambrooke Leigh 103
    Lesson 24. "Jabberwocky" by Lewis Carroll 107

PART VII. ALLUSION 111
    Lesson 25. "Fire and Ice" by Robert Frost 112
    Lesson 26. "The World Is Too Much with Us" by William Wordsworth 116
    Lesson 27. "Christmas Day" by Christina Rossetti 120
    Lesson 28. "The Lady of Shalott" by Alfred Lord Tennyson 124

PART VIII. HYPERBOLE **130**

Lesson 29. "Concord Hymn" by Ralph Waldo Emerson 131
Lesson 30. "A Red, Red Rose" by Robert Burns 135
Lesson 31. "Casey at the Bat" by Ernest Lawrence Thayer........................... 139
Lesson 32. "For Each Ecstatic Instant" by Emily Dickinson 144

PART IX. ONOMATOPOEIA...**148**

Lesson 33. "The Bells" by Edgar Allan Poe... 149
Lesson 34. "Meeting at Night" by Robert Browning 158
Lesson 35. "Gathering Leaves" by Robert Frost 162
Lesson 36. "I heard a Fly buzz – when I died" by Emily Dickinson 166

LESSON ANSWERS..170
REFERENCES AND ADDITIONAL READING 184

Goals of This Book Series

This book series aims to familiarize children with works of poetry from an early age, nurture the imagination, inspire an appreciation for beauty, encourage a mind for symbolism and nuance, foster the ability to narrate complex ideas, and expand children's vocabularies. Lessons are short and interactive by design to target elementary school-aged children.

Inspiration for This Book Series

Charlotte Mason, born in 1842, sought to provide teaching advice and strategies to instructors and homeschooling parents. She detailed her educational philosophies and methodologies in her multi-volume *Home Education Series*. She advocated for centering instruction around living works, such as the finest art, music, poetry, and prose. Mason recommended that from an early age, children engage in the regular study of poetry, including reciting poetry. In her *Home Education Series*, she writes, "…include a good deal of poetry, to accustom him to the delicate rendering of shades of meaning, and especially to make him aware that words are beautiful in themselves, that they are a source of pleasure, and are worthy of our honour; and that a beautiful word deserves to be beautifully said, with a certain roundness of tone and precision of utterance."

The Targeted Audience for This Book

This book targets elementary school-aged children in grades four and up.

Overview of This Book

This book provides 36 lessons or enough for one lesson per week over a standard 36-week school year. This volume overviews nine literary devices: 1) Rhyming, 2) Alliteration, 3) Simile, 4) Metaphor, 5) Personification, 6) Foreshadowing, 7) Allusion, 8) Hyperbole, and 9) Onomatopoeia. This course incorporates poetry, narration, copywork, dictation, device identification, device employment, and artwork. Featured poets include Christina Rossetti, Paul Laurence Dunbar, Alfred Lord Tennyson, William Wordsworth, Robert Frost, and Emily Dickinson.

How to Teach Using This Book

The tables below outline the recommended instructional approach to teach a 36-week course using this book.

Every Four Weeks – Introduce a New Literary Device	
Section Title	**Section Instructions**
Introduction	<ul><li>Instructors overview the nine literary devices with students.</li><li>Instructors introduce the featured literary device to students.</li><li>Instructors and students review any provided examples.</li></ul>

Every Week – Introduce a New Poem	
Section Title	**Section Instructions**
Featured Poem	<ul><li>Students study one poem per week over the 36-week school year.</li><li>Students recite the poem line by line with instructor assistance.</li></ul>
Synopsis	Students read the summary of the poem.
Recite Poem, Title, and Poet	Students practice reciting the poem, the poem title, and the poet name.
Narrate the Poem	Students write a summary of the poem in their own words.
Complete Copywork	Students copy the provided poem excerpt.
Complete Dictations	Instructors recite the excerpt, and students write the words as they are spoken.
Device Identification and Employment	<ul><li>Students examine use of literary devices in lesson poems.</li><li>Students review instances of previously featured literary devices.</li><li>Students employ literary devices to compose their own poems.</li></ul>
Create Novel Artwork	Students generate unique art based on the poem or literary device.

PART I: RHYMING

INTRODUCTION

This book introduces nine common literary devices. Poets often employ literary devices, defined as "rules of thumb, convention, or structure that are employed in literature and storytelling." The list below enumerates the nine literary devices covered in this book. The first four lessons in this book focus on the sublime use of rhyme.

1. **Rhyming**
2. Alliteration
3. Simile
4. Metaphor
5. Personification
6. Foreshadowing
7. Allusion
8. Hyperbole
9. Onomatopoeia

Rhyming is defined as "a word that is pronounced identically with another word from the vowel in its stressed syllable to the end." A rhyme scheme is defined as "the pattern created by the rhymes at the ends of the lines of a stanza of poetry."

1. Study the poem, "Little Miss Muffet," by Mother Goose, and identify the pairs of rhyming words.
2. Note the rhyme scheme of A-A-B-C-C-B.

Rhyme Scheme	Poem Line
A	Little Miss Muffet
A	Sat on a tuffet,
B	Eating her curds and whey;
C	Along came a spider,
C	Who sat down beside her,
B	And frightened Miss Muffet away.

Review the common rhyme schemes:
- Traditional: A-B-A-B...
- Couplet: A-A-B-B...
- Enclosed: A-B-B-A...
- Triplet: A-A-A-B-B-B...

LESSON 1: "REMEMBER"
BY CHRISTINA ROSSETTI (RHYMING)

FEATURED POEM

Remember me when I am gone away,
    Gone far away into the silent land;
    When you can no more hold me by the hand,
Nor I half turn to go yet turning stay.
Remember me when no more day by day
    You tell me of our future that you plann'd:
    Only remember me; you understand
It will be late to counsel then or pray.
Yet if you should forget me for a while
    And afterwards remember, do not grieve:
    For if the darkness and corruption leave
    A vestige of the thoughts that once I had,
Better by far you should forget and smile
    Than that you should remember and be sad.

SYNOPSIS

In the poem title, the narrator asks the reader to remember something. The poem reveals that the narrator fears dying and leaving their loved one. The first eight lines plead with the reader not to forget to narrator. The remaining lines comfort the reader, asking that if the reader temporarily forgets and then remembers the narrator, not to feel guilty, but to be happy. The narrator expresses trepidation over where our spirits venture after death, referring to the "silent land" and "darkness and corruption." Note how the poet rhymes the last word of each line for effect.

RECITE POEM, TITLE, AND POET

Practice reciting the poem, the poem title, and the name of the poet.

NARRATE THE POEM

_____

_____

_____

_____

_____

_____

_____

_____

_____

COMPLETE COPYWORK

Remember me when I am gone away,
Gone far away into the silent land;

_____

_____

_____

ELEMENTARY POETRY VOLUME 5: LITERARY DEVICES

COMPLETE DICTATION

_____

_____

_____

DEVICE IDENTIFICATION AND EMPLOYMENT

1. Examine the rhyming scheme in the Mother Goose poem, "Humpty Dumpty."

   Humpty Dumpty sat on a wall
   Humpty Dumpty had a great fall.
   All the king's horses and all the king's men
   Couldn't put Humpty together again.

   Does the poem follow a traditional (ABAB), couplet (AABB), enclosed (ABBA), or triplet (AAABBB) rhyming scheme?

   _____

2. Study the poem and assign letters (A, B, ...) to the rhyming words to reveal the rhyming scheme.

Remember me when I am gone away,	( )
Gone far away into the silent land;	( )
When you can no more hold me by the hand,	( )
Nor I half turn to go yet turning stay.	( )
Remember me when no more day by day	( )
You tell me of our future that you plann'd:	( )
Only remember me; you understand	( )
It will be late to counsel then or pray.	( )
Yet if you should forget me for a while	( )
And afterwards remember, do not grieve:	( )
For if the darkness and corruption leave	( )
A vestige of the thoughts that once I had,	( )
Better by far you should forget and smile	( )
Than that you should remember and be sad.	( )

   Do the first eight lines of the poem follow a traditional (ABAB), couplet (AABB), enclosed (ABBA), or triplet (AAABBB) rhyming scheme?

   _____

3. Write a poem of four lines, employing the traditional rhyming scheme, A-B-A-B.

    _____ (A)

    _____ (B)

    _____ (A)

    _____ (B)

CREATE NOVEL ARTWORK (Sketch something you would like to remember for all time.)

LESSON 2: "ALL THINGS BRIGHT AND BEAUTIFUL" BY CECIL FRANCES ALEXANDER (RHYMING)

FEATURED POEM

1. All things bright and beautiful,
All creatures great and small,
All things wise and wonderful,
The Lord God made them all.

2. Each little flower that opens,
Each little bird that sings,
He made their glowing colors,
He made their tiny wings.

3. The rich man in his castle,
The poor man at his gate,
God made them, high or lowly,
And ordered their estate.

4. The purple-headed mountain,
The river running by,
The morning and the sunset,
That lighted up the sky.

5. The cold wind in the winter,
The pleasant summer sun,
The ripe fruits in the garden,
He made them every one.

6. The tall trees in the greenwood,
The meadows where we play,
The rushes by the water,
We gather every day.

7. He gave us eyes to see them,
And lips that we might tell,
How great is God Almighty,
Who has made all things well.

SYNOPSIS

"All Things Bright and Beautiful" is a Christian hymn written in 1848 by Cecil Frances Alexander. The poetic text has been set to different melodies over the years. The text praises God for the brightness and beauty of the world, including flowers, birds, people from all walks of life, mountains, rivers, and trees. The text employs rhyming as a poetic device for effect.

RECITE POEM, TITLE, AND POET

Practice reciting the poem, the poem title, and the name of the poet.

NARRATE THE POEM

_____

_____

_____

_____

_____

_____

_____

COMPLETE COPYWORK

The purple-headed mountain,
The river running by,
The morning and the sunset,
That lighted up the sky;

_____

_____

_____

COMPLETE DICTATION

_____

_____

_____

_____

DEVICE IDENTIFICATION AND EMPLOYMENT

1. Examine the rhyming scheme in the Mother Goose poem, "Bees."

    A swarm of bees in May
    Is worth a load of hay;
    A swarm of bees in June
    Is worth a silver spoon;
    A swarm of bees in July
    Is not worth a fly.

    Does the poem follow a traditional (ABAB), couplet (AABB), enclosed (ABBA), or triplet (AAABBB) rhyming scheme?

    _____

2. Study the poem excerpt and assign letters to the rhyming words to reveal the rhyming scheme.

Each little flower that opens,	( )
Each little bird that sings,	( )
He made their glowing colors,	( )
He made their tiny wings.	( )
The rich man in his castle,	( )
The poor man at his gate,	( )
God made them, high or lowly,	( )
And ordered their estate.	( )

3. Write a poem of four lines, employing the couplet rhyming scheme, A-A-B-B.

　　_____ (A)

　　_____ (A)

　　_____ (B)

　　_____ (B)

CREATE NOVEL ARTWORK (Draw something you find "bright and beautiful.")

LESSON 3: "CHRISTMAS CAROL"
BY PAUL LAURENCE DUNBAR (RHYMING)

FEATURED POEM

1. Ring out, ye bells!
   All Nature swells
  With gladness at the wondrous story,
   The world was lorn,
   But Christ is born
  To change our sadness into glory.

2. Sing, earthlings, sing!
   To-night a King
  Hath come from heaven's high throne to bless us.
   The outstretched hand
   O'er all the land
  Is raised in pity to caress us.

3. Come at his call;
   Be joyful all;
  Away with mourning and with sadness!
   The heavenly choir
   With holy fire
  Their voices raise in songs of gladness.

4. The darkness breaks
   And Dawn awakes,
  Her cheeks suffused with youthful blushes.
   The rocks and stones
   In holy tones
  Are singing sweeter than the thrushes.

5. Then why should we
   In silence be,
  When Nature lends her voice to praises;
   When heaven and earth
   Proclaim the truth
  Of Him for whom that lone star blazes?

6. No, be not still,
   But with a will
  Strike all your harps and set them ringing;
   On hill and heath
   Let every breath
  Throw all its power into singing!

SYNOPSIS

Paul Laurence Dunbar's "Christmas Carol" celebrates Christmas and the birth of Jesus Christ from the Christian Bible. The poem employs the literary device of rhyming.

RECITE POEM, TITLE, AND POET

Practice reciting the poem, the poem title, and the name of the poet.

NARRATE THE POEM

_____

_____

_____

_____

_____

COMPLETE COPYWORK

Ring out, ye bells!
All Nature swells
With gladness at the wondrous story,
To change our sadness into glory.

_____

_____

_____

_____

ELEMENTARY POETRY VOLUME 5: LITERARY DEVICES

COMPLETE DICTATION

_____

_____

_____

_____

DEVICE IDENTIFICATION AND EMPLOYMENT

1. Examine the rhyming scheme in the Mother Goose poem, "Heigh-Ho, The Carrion Crow."

    A carrion crow sat on an oak,
    Fol de riddle, lol de riddle, hi ding doe,
    Watching a tailor shape his cloak
    Sing heigh-ho, the carrion crow.

    Does the poem follow a traditional (ABAB), couplet (AABB), enclosed (ABBA), or triplet (AAABBB) rhyming scheme?

    _____

2. Study the poem excerpt and assign letters to the rhyming words to reveal the rhyming scheme.

Ring out, ye bells!	( )
All Nature swells	( )
With gladness at the wondrous story,	( )
The world was lorn,	( )
But Christ is born	( )
To change our sadness into glory.	( )
The darkness breaks.	( )
And Dawn awakes,	( )
Her cheeks suffused with youthful blushes.	( )
The rocks and stones.	( )
In holy tones.	( )
Are singing sweeter than the thrushes.	( )

3. Write a poem of six lines, employing the triplet rhyming scheme, A-A-A-B-B-B.

_____ (A)

_____ (A)

_____ (A)

_____ (B)

_____ (B)

_____ (B)

CREATE NOVEL ARTWORK (Illustrate what Christmas or another special holiday means to you.)

ELEMENTARY POETRY VOLUME 5: LITERARY DEVICES

LESSON 4: "MERRY AUTUMN"
BY PAUL LAURENCE DUNBAR (RHYMING)

FEATURED POEM

1. It's all a farce,—these tales they tell
   About the breezes sighing,
And moans astir o'er field and dell,
   Because the year is dying.

2. Such principles are most absurd,
   I care not who first taught 'em;
There's nothing known to beast or bird
   To make a solemn autumn.

3. In solemn times, when grief holds sway
   With countenance distressing,
You'll note the more of black and gray
   Will then be used in dressing.

4. Now purple tints are all around;
   The sky is blue and mellow;
And e'en the grasses turn the ground
   From modest green to yellow.

5. The seed burrs all with laughter crack
   On featherweed and jimson;
And leaves that should be dressed in black
   Are all decked out in crimson.

6. A butterfly goes winging by;
   A singing bird comes after;
And Nature, all from earth to sky,
   Is bubbling o'er with laughter.

7. The ripples wimple on the rills,
   Like sparkling little lasses;
The sunlight runs along the hills,
   And laughs among the grasses.

8. The earth is just so full of fun
   It really can't contain it;
And streams of mirth so freely run
   The heavens seem to rain it.

9. Don't talk to me of solemn days
   In autumn's time of splendor,
Because the sun shows fewer rays,
   And these grow slant and slender.

10. Why, it's the climax of the year,
    The highest time of living!
Till naturally its bursting cheer
    Just melts into thanksgiving.

SYNOPSIS

In "Merry Autumn," Paul Laurence Dunbar scolds those who mourn autumn and the "dying of the year." Dunbar argues that autumn is a glorious time of reds and yellows, singing birds, sunshine, and fun. Dunbar sees autumn as the very best of the seasons and the "climax of the year."

RECITE POEM, TITLE, AND POET

Practice reciting the poem, the poem title, and the name of the poet.

NARRATE THE POEM

_____

_____

_____

_____

COMPLETE COPYWORK

Why, it's the climax of the year,
The highest time of living!
Till naturally its bursting cheer
Just melts into thanksgiving.

_____

_____

_____

_____

ELEMENTARY POETRY VOLUME 5: LITERARY DEVICES

COMPLETE DICTATION

_____

_____

_____

_____

DEVICE IDENTIFICATION AND EMPLOYMENT

1. Study the rhyming scheme in John Milton's poem, "How Soon Hath Time."

   How soon hath Time, the subtle thief of youth,
   Stolen on his wing my three and twentieth year!
   My hasting days fly on with full career
   But my late spring no bud or blossom shew'th.

   Does the poem follow a traditional (ABAB), couplet (AABB), enclosed (ABBA), or triplet (AAABBB) rhyming scheme?

   _____

2. Examine the poem excerpt and assign letters to the rhyming words to reveal the rhyming scheme.

The earth is just so full of fun	( )
It really can't contain it;	( )
And streams of mirth so freely run	( )
The heavens seem to rain it.	( )
Don't talk to me of solemn days	( )
In autumn's time of splendor,	( )
Because the sun shows fewer rays,	( )
And these grow slant and slender.	( )
Why, it's the climax of the year,—	( )
The highest time of living!—	( )
Till naturally its bursting cheer	( )
Just melts into thanksgiving.	( )

3. Write a poem of four lines, employing the enclosed rhyming scheme, A-B-B-A.

   _____ (A)

   _____ (B)

   _____ (B)

   _____ (A)

CREATE NOVEL ARTWORK (Draw your favorite aspect of autumn.)

ELEMENTARY POETRY VOLUME 5: LITERARY DEVICES

PART II: ALLITERATION

INTRODUCTION

Recall that literary devices are defined as "rules of thumb, convention, or structure that are employed in literature and storytelling." The next four lessons address the alluring allocation of alliteration in poetry.

1. Rhyming
2. **Alliteration**
3. Simile
4. Metaphor
5. Personification
6. Foreshadowing
7. Allusion
8. Hyperbole
9. Onomatopoeia

Alliteration is defined as the "repetition of consonant sounds at the beginning of two or more words in a row, or at short intervals."

1. Review the poem, "Three Gray Geese" and its instances of alliteration.
2. Note the alliteration of the sounds of "G," "R," and "GR."
3. The left image marks all words starting with a "G" sound.
4. The right image marks all words starting with an "R" sound.

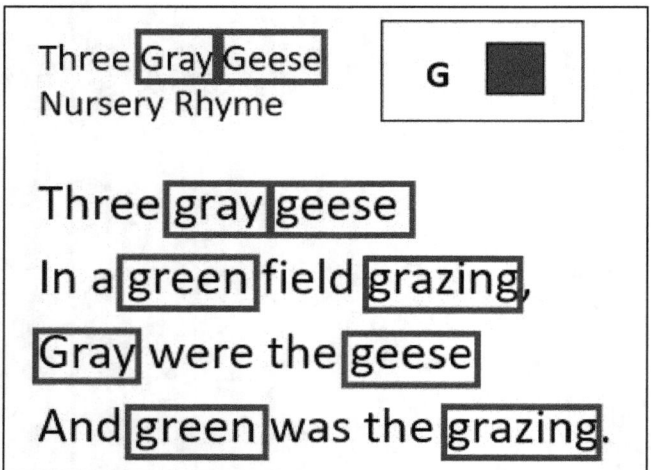 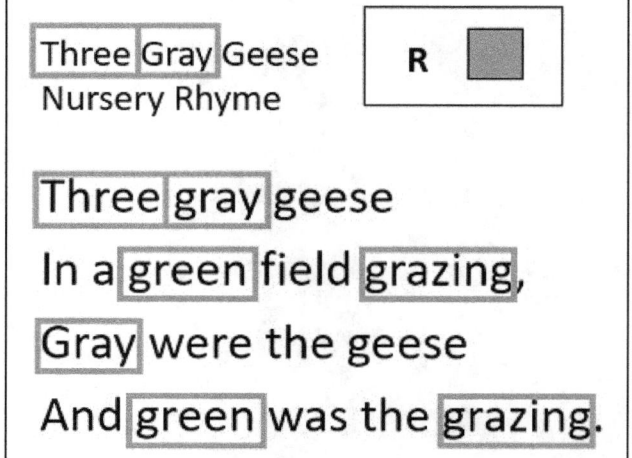

LESSON 5: "THE BUTTER BETTY BOUGHT" BY CAROLYN WELLS (ALLITERATION)

FEATURED POEM

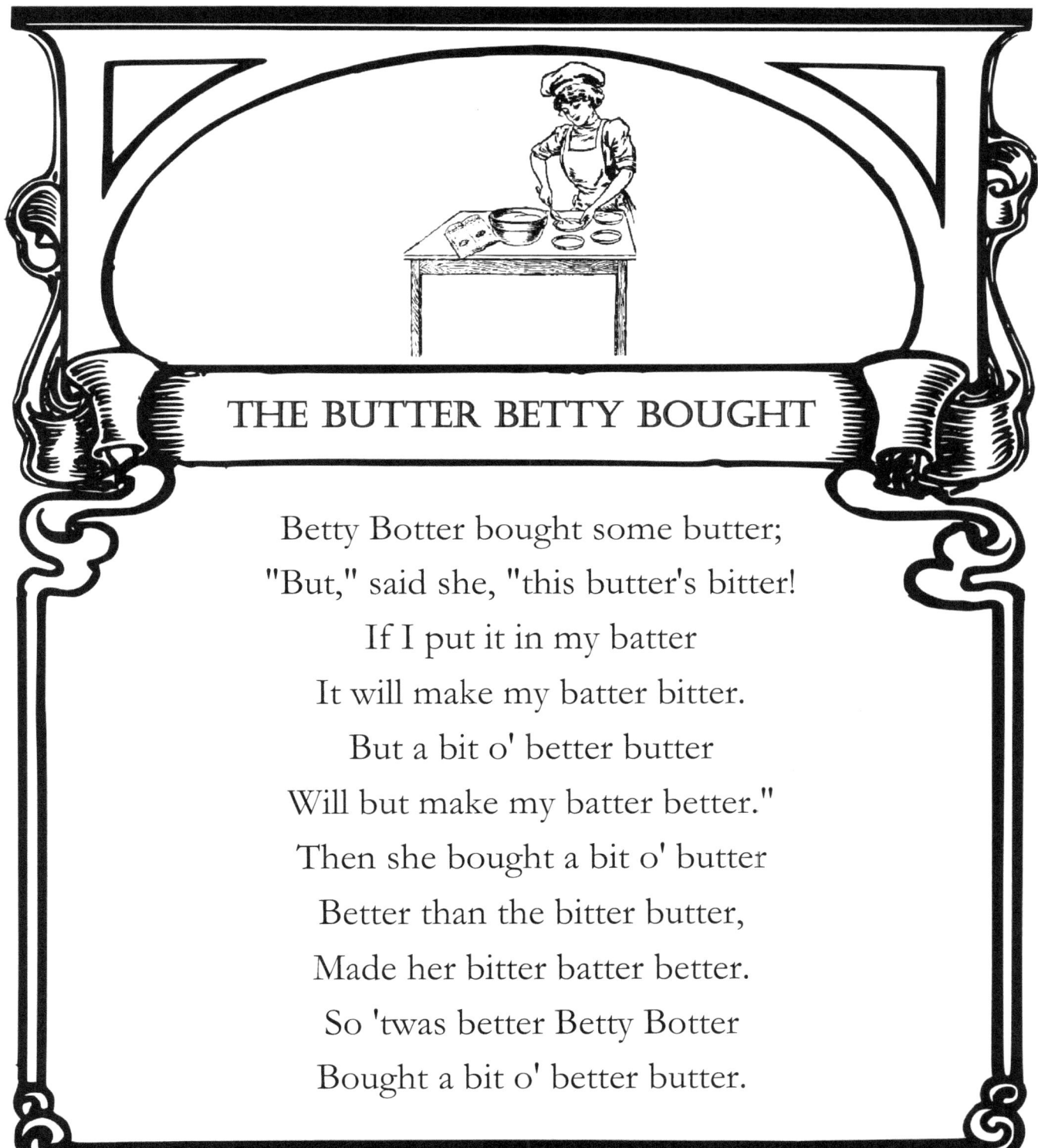

THE BUTTER BETTY BOUGHT

Betty Botter bought some butter;
"But," said she, "this butter's bitter!
If I put it in my batter
It will make my batter bitter.
But a bit o' better butter
Will but make my batter better."
Then she bought a bit o' butter
Better than the bitter butter,
Made her bitter batter better.
So 'twas better Betty Botter
Bought a bit o' better butter.

SYNOPSIS

"The Butter Betty Bought" by Carolyn Wells plays with alliteration to create a fun tongue-twister. Poor Betty has bitter butter that will blemish her batter. She runs out to pick up some preferable butter to make her batter better.

RECITE POEM, TITLE, AND POET

Practice reciting the poem, the poem title, and the name of the poet.

NARRATE THE POEM

_____

_____

_____

_____

COMPLETE COPYWORK

Betty Botter bought some butter;
"But," said she, "this butter's bitter!
If I put it in my batter
It will make my batter bitter."

_____

_____

_____

COMPLETE DICTATION

_____

_____

_____

_____

DEVICE IDENTIFICATION AND EMPLOYMENT

1. Study a Tongue-twister

    - Tongue-twisters are "phrases that are deliberately designed to be difficult to say correctly, usually because of varying combinations of similar sounds."
    - See how fast you can recite the tongue-twister, "Peter Piper."
    - Identify and circle any instances of alliteration.

    Peter Piper picked a peck of pickled peppers.

    A peck of pickled peppers Peter Piper picked.

    If Peter Piper picked a peck of pickled peppers,

    Where's the peck of pickled peppers Peter Piper picked?

2. Circle the words starting with a "B" sound to reveal the use of alliteration.

    Betty Botter bought some butter;

    "But," said she, "this butter's bitter!

    If I put it in my batter

    It will make my batter bitter.

    But a bit o' better butter

    Will but make my batter better."

    Then she bought a bit o' butter

    Better than the bitter butter,

    Made her bitter batter better.

3. Write a poem of four lines, employing alliteration using the sound of the letter "B."

_____ (B)

_____ (B)

_____ (B)

_____ (B)

CREATE NOVEL ARTWORK (Invent a new tongue-twister and create an illustration to accompany it.)

Tongue-twister:
Illustration:

LESSON 6: "THE SIEGE OF BELGRADE" BY ALARIC ALEXANDER WATTS (ALLITERATION)

FEATURED POEM

An Austrian army, awfully arrayed,

Boldly by battery besieged Belgrade.

Cossack commanders cannonading come,

Dealing destruction's devastating doom.

Every endeavor engineers essay,

For fame, for fortune fighting - furious fray!

Generals 'gainst generals grapple - gracious God!

How honors Heaven heroic hardihood!

Infuriate, indiscriminate in ill,

Jostle John Jarovlitz, Jem, Joe, Jack, Jill:

Kindred kill kinsmen, kinsmen kindred kill.

Labor low levels longest, loftiest lines;

Men march 'mid mounds, 'mid moles, 'mid murderous mines;

Now noxious, noisy numbers nothing, naught

Of outward obstacles, opposing ought;

Poor patriots, partly purchased, partly pressed,

Quite quaking, quickly "Quarter! Quarter!" quest.

Reason returns, religious right redounds,

Suwarrow stops such sanguinary sounds.

Truce to thee, Turkey! Triumph to thy train,

Unwise, unjust, unmerciful Ukraine!

Vanish vain victory! vanish, victory vain!

Why wish we warfare? Wherefore welcome were

Xerxes, Ximenes, Xanthus, Xavier?

Yield, yield, ye youths! ye yeomen, yield your yell!

Zeus', Zarpater's, Zoroaster's zeal,

Attracting all, arms against acts appeal!

SYNOPSIS

Alaric Alexander Watts takes alliteration to the extreme in his poem, "The Siege of Belgrade." Each line corresponds to one letter in the alphabet, with the letter "A" repeating at the end. The poem describes the 1789 siege in which the Austrian army besieged a Turkish force sheltering within the fortress of Belgrade in modern-day Serbia. After three weeks, the Turkish forces surrendered. Today, Belgrade is the name of the capital of Serbia.

RECITE POEM, TITLE, AND POET

Practice reciting the poem, the poem title, and the name of the poet.

NARRATE THE POEM

_____

_____

_____

COMPLETE COPYWORK

An Austrian army, awfully arrayed,
Boldly by battery besieged Belgrade.
Cossack commanders cannonading come,
Dealing destruction's devastating doom.

_____

_____

_____

COMPLETE DICTATION

_____

_____

_____

_____

DEVICE IDENTIFICATION AND EMPLOYMENT

1. Study a Tongue-twister

    - Recite the tongue-twister.
    - Circle alliterative instances of "s" sounds in red and "sh" sounds in blue.

    She sells seashells by the seashore.

    The shells she sells are surely seashells.

    So if she sells shells on the seashore,

    I'm sure she sells seashore shells.

2. Identify the Rhyme Scheme

    a. Circle words starting with the indicated letter sounds to reveal the use of alliteration.
    b. Assign letters to the sentences to reveal the rhyming scheme.

Alliteration Sounds		**Rhyming Scheme** (e.g. A-A-B-B)
(A)	An Austrian army, awfully arrayed,	( )
(B)	Boldly by battery besieged Belgrade.	( )
(C)	Cossack commanders cannonading come,	( )
(D)	Dealing destruction's devastating doom.	( )
(E)	Every endeavor engineers essay,	( )
(F)	For fame, for fortune fighting - furious fray!	( )
(G)	Generals 'gainst generals grapple - gracious God!	( )
(H)	How honors Heaven heroic hardihood!	( )

3. Write a poem of four lines, employing alliteration of the letters, A, B, C, and D, as indicated.

_____ (A)

_____ (B)

_____ (C)

_____ (D)

CREATE NOVEL ARTWORK (Illustrate something that literally or figuratively represents a battle.)

LESSON 7: "THE EAGLE"
BY ALFRED LORD TENNYSON (ALLITERATION)

FEATURED POEM

He clasps the crag with crooked hands;

Close to the sun in lonely lands,

Ring'd with the azure world, he stands.

The wrinkled sea beneath him crawls;

He watches from his mountain walls,

And like a thunderbolt he falls.

SYNOPSIS

Alfred Lord Tennyson's "The Eagle" sprinkles alliteration throughout the poem for effect. The poem details a lone eagle surveying the land and sea from his craggy perch. The eagle launches himself and rockets down from the mountaintop.

RECITE POEM, TITLE, AND POET

Practice reciting the poem, the poem title, and the name of the poet.

NARRATE THE POEM

_____

_____

_____

_____

_____

COMPLETE COPYWORK

He clasps the crag with crooked hands;
Close to the sun in lonely lands,
Ring'd with the azure world, he stands.

_____

_____

_____

_____

COMPLETE DICTATION

_____

_____

_____

_____

DEVICE IDENTIFICATION AND EMPLOYMENT

1. Study a Tongue-twister

    - Recite the tongue-twister.
    - Circle alliterative instances of "w" sounds in red, "ch" in blue, and "ould/ood" in green.

    How much wood would a woodchuck chuck if a woodchuck could chuck wood?

2. Identify the Rhyme Scheme
    a. Circle words starting with the indicated letter sounds to reveal the use of alliteration.
    b. Assign letters to the sentences to reveal the rhyming scheme.

Alliteration Sounds		**Rhyming Scheme** (e.g. A-A-B-B)
(C)	He clasps the crag with crooked hands;	( )
(L)	Close to the sun in lonely lands,	( )
	Ring'd with the azure world, he stands.	( )
	The wrinkled sea beneath him crawls;	( )
(W)	He watches from his mountain walls,	( )
	And like a thunderbolt he falls.	( )

Does the poem follow a traditional (ABAB), couplet (AABB), enclosed (ABBA), or triplet (AAABBB) rhyming scheme?

_____

3. Write a poem of four lines that exemplifies alliteration. Write the alliterative letter after each line.

_____ ( )

_____ ( )

_____ ( )

_____ ( )

CREATE NOVEL ARTWORK (Sketch the viewpoint of the eagle as he soars above the earth.)

LESSON 8: "PIED BEAUTY"
BY GERARD MANLEY HOPKINS (ALLITERATION)

FEATURED POEM

Glory be to God for dappled things –
   For skies of couple-color as a brinded cow;
     For rose-moles all in stipple upon trout that swim;
Fresh-firecoal chestnut-falls; finches' wings;
   Landscape plotted and pieced – fold, fallow, and plough;
   And all trades, their gear and tackle and trim.

All things counter, original, spare, strange;
   Whatever is fickle, freckled (who knows how?)
   With swift, slow; sweet, sour; adazzle, dim;
He fathers-forth whose beauty is past change:
   Praise him.

SYNOPSIS

In Gerard Manley Hopkins' "Pied Beauty," he praises God for multicolored (pied) things, including the sky, cows, chestnuts, trout, finches, and farmland. He also thanks God for freckled things not typically thought of as beautiful - the odd and the strange. Note the instances of alliteration and the use of indentation to indicate the rhyme scheme.

RECITE POEM, TITLE, AND POET

Practice reciting the poem, the poem title, and the name of the poet.

NARRATE THE POEM

_____

_____

_____

_____

COMPLETE COPYWORK

Glory be to God for dappled things —
　For skies of couple-color as a brinded cow;
　　For rose-moles all in stipple upon trout that swim;
Fresh-firecoal chestnut-falls; finches' wings;

_____

_____

_____

_____

COMPLETE DICTATION

_____

_____

_____

_____

_____

DEVICE IDENTIFICATION AND EMPLOYMENT

1. Study a Tongue-twister

    - Recite the tongue-twister.
    - Circle alliterative instances of "s" sounds in red and "sh" sounds in blue.

    Silly Sally swiftly shooed seven silly sheep.
    The seven silly sheep Silly Sally shooed
    Shillyshallied south.

2. Identify the Rhyme Scheme
    a. Circle words starting with the indicated letter sounds to reveal the use of alliteration.
    b. Assign letters to the sentences to reveal the rhyming scheme.

Alliteration Sounds		**Rhyming Scheme** (e.g. A-A-B-B)
(G)	Glory be to God for dappled things –	( )
(C)	For skies of couple-color as a brinded cow;	( )
	For rose-moles all in stipple upon trout that swim;	( )
(F)	Fresh-firecoal chestnut-falls; finches' wings;	( )
(P/F)	Landscape plotted and pieced – fold, fallow, and plough;	( )
	And all trades, their gear and tackle and trim.	( )
(S)	All things counter, original, spare, strange;	( )
(F)	Whatever is fickle, freckled (who knows how?)	( )
(S/D)	With swift, slow; sweet, sour; adazzle, dim;	( )
(F)	He fathers-forth whose beauty is past change:	( )
	Praise him.	( )

3. Write a poem of six lines that exemplifies alliteration. Write the alliterative letter after each line.

_____ ( )

_____ ( )

_____ ( )

_____ ( )

_____ ( )

_____ ( )

CREATE NOVEL ARTWORK (Sketch a pied object or animal.)

PART III: SIMILE

INTRODUCTION

Recall that literary devices are defined as "rules of thumb, convention, or structure that are employed in literature and storytelling." Poetry featured in the next four lessons drip similes like a leaky faucet.

1. Rhyming
2. Alliteration
3. **Simile**
4. Metaphor
5. Personification
6. Foreshadowing
7. Allusion
8. Hyperbole
9. Onomatopoeia

Similes are figures of speech comparing two things, generally using "like" or "as." Study the poem excerpt from "Mary Had a Little Lamb" by Mother Goose and identify the simile.

> Simile Clues – "As" and "Like"
>
> Mary had a little lamb,
> Little lamb, little lamb,
> Mary had a little lamb
> Whose fleece was white as snow.

Which two items are compared using a simile and the word "as" in the poem, "Mary Had a Little Lamb?"

Item #1: _____

Item #2: _____

What do the two items have in common? _____

LESSON 9: "A VISIT FROM ST. NICHOLAS" BY CLEMENT CLARKE MOORE (SIMILE)

FEATURED POEM

'Twas the night before Christmas, when all through the house
Not a creature was stirring, not even a mouse;
The stockings were hung by the chimney with care,
In hopes that St. Nicholas soon would be there;

The children were nestled all snug in their beds,
While visions of sugar-plums danced in their heads;
And mamma in her 'kerchief, and I in my cap,
Had just settled our brains for a long winter's nap,

When out on the lawn there arose such a clatter,
I sprang from the bed to see what was the matter.
Away to the window I flew like a flash,
Tore open the shutters and threw up the sash.

The moon on the breast of the new-fallen snow
Gave the luster of midday to objects below,
When, what to my wondering eyes should appear,
But a miniature sleigh, and eight tiny reindeer,

With a little old driver, so lively and quick,
I knew in a moment it must be St. Nick.
More rapid than eagles his coursers they came,
And he whistled, and shouted, and called them by name;

"Now, Dasher! now, Dancer! now, Prancer and Vixen!
On, Comet! on, Cupid! on, Donder and Blitzen!
To the top of the porch! to the top of the wall!
Now dash away! dash away! dash away all!"

As dry leaves that before the wild hurricane fly,
When they meet with an obstacle, mount to the sky;
So up to the house-top the coursers they flew,
With the sleigh full of Toys, and St. Nicholas too.

And then, in a twinkling, I heard on the roof
The prancing and pawing of each little hoof.
As I drew in my head, and was turning around,
Down the chimney St. Nicholas came with a bound.

He was dressed all in fur, from his head to his foot,
And his clothes were all tarnished with ashes and soot;
A bundle of toys he had flung on his back,
And he looked like a peddler just opening his pack.

His eyes—how they twinkled! his dimples how merry!
His cheeks were like roses, his nose like a cherry!
His droll little mouth was drawn up like a bow
And the beard of his chin was as white as the snow;

The stump of a pipe he held tight in his teeth,
And the smoke it encircled his head like a wreath;
He had a broad face and a little round belly,
That shook when he laughed, like a bowlful of jelly.

He was chubby and plump, a right jolly old elf.
And I laughed when I saw him, in spite of myself;
A wink of his eye and a twist of his head,
Soon gave me to know I had nothing to dread:

He spoke not a word, but went straight to his work,
And filled all the stockings; then turned with a jerk,
And laying his finger aside of his nose,
And giving a nod, up the chimney he rose;

He sprang to his sleigh, to his team gave a whistle,
And away they all flew like the down of a thistle,
But I heard him exclaim, ere he drove out of sight,
"Happy Christmas to all, and to all a good-night."

SYNOPSIS

The beloved classic, "A Visit from St Nicholas," by Clement Clarke Moore is read in many American homes on Christmas Eve. In the poem, the father of the family is awakened by the arrival of Santa Claus and his reindeer. The father watches as Santa Claus comes down the chimney and marvels at Santa's jolly features and demeanor. Santa Claus fills the stockings, vanishes back up the chimney, and calls out "Happy Christmas to all, and to all a good-night" as his sleigh soars away through the air. The poem contains multiple similes, particularly while describing Santa Claus.

RECITE POEM, TITLE, AND POET

Practice reciting the poem, the poem title, and the name of the poet.

NARRATE THE POEM

_____

_____

_____

_____

_____

_____

_____

COMPLETE COPYWORK

'Twas the night before Christmas,
when all through the house
Not a creature was stirring, not even a mouse;

_____

_____

_____

_____

ELEMENTARY POETRY VOLUME 5: LITERARY DEVICES

COMPLETE DICTATION

_____

_____

_____

_____

DEVICE IDENTIFICATION AND EMPLOYMENT

1. Recognize Use of Similes
   - Recite the sentences.
   - Circle the simile clues in each sentence – "as" or "like."
     a. The kite soared like a bird.
     b. Her sunburned shoulders felt as hot and dry as a desert.
     c. He was cold as ice.
     d. His face was red like a tomato.
     e. She was as fast as the wind.

2. Review the poem and identify a few examples of alliteration

3. Identify the Similes and Rhyming Scheme
   a. Circle the similes in the poem excerpt.
   b. Assign letters to the sentences to reveal the rhyming scheme.

Rhyming Scheme (e.g. A-A-B-B)

A bundle of toys he had flung on his back,	( )
And he looked like a peddler just opening his pack.	( )
His eyes—how they twinkled! his dimples how merry!	( )
His cheeks were like roses, his nose like a cherry!	( )
His droll little mouth was drawn up like a bow	( )
And the beard of his chin was as white as the snow;	( )
The stump of a pipe he held tight in his teeth,	( )
And the smoke it encircled his head like a wreath;	( )
He had a broad face and a little round belly,	( )
That shook when he laughed, like a bowlful of jelly.	( )

4. Complete the similes.

   a. The man was as enormous as _____.

   b. The girl sang like _____.

   c. The wolf revealed teeth as sharp as _____.

   d. The baby's cheeks were soft like _____.

CREATE NOVEL ARTWORK (Sketch something related to Santa Claus or another holiday figure.)

ELEMENTARY POETRY VOLUME 5: LITERARY DEVICES

LESSON 10: "A LADY"
BY AMY LOWELL (SIMILE)

FEATURED POEM

You are beautiful and faded,

Like an old opera tune

Played upon a harpsichord;

Or like the sun-flooded silks

Of an eighteenth-century boudoir.

In your eyes

Smolder the fallen roses of outlived minutes,

And the perfume of your soul

Is vague and suffusing,

With the pungence of sealed spice-jars.

Your half-tones delight me,

And I grow mad with gazing

At your blent colors.

My vigor is a new-minted penny,

Which I cast at your feet.

Gather it up from the dust

That its sparkle may amuse you.

SYNOPSIS

The young narrator in Amy Lowell's "A Lady," employs similes to describe their fascination with the faded beauty of an older woman. The narrator entertains the older woman with their active and youthful behavior.

RECITE POEM, TITLE, AND POET

Practice reciting the poem, the poem title, and the name of the poet.

NARRATE THE POEM

COMPLETE COPYWORK

You are beautiful and faded,
Like an old opera tune
Played upon a harpsichord;

ELEMENTARY POETRY VOLUME 5: LITERARY DEVICES

COMPLETE DICTATION

_____

_____

_____

_____

_____

DEVICE IDENTIFICATION AND EMPLOYMENT

1. Recognize Use of Similes
   - Recite the sentences.
   - Circle the simile clues in each sentence – "as" or "like."
      a. Her skin was as rough as sandpaper.
      b. The fabric was soft like a bunny.
      c. The stew was as spicy as a jalapeno.
      d. Her smile was as sweet as a lollipop.
      e. His words cut like a knife.

2. Find the Similes
   Study the poem excerpt and circle the similes.

   > You are beautiful and faded,
   > Like an old opera tune
   > Played upon a harpsichord;
   > Or like the sun-flooded silks
   > Of an eighteenth-century boudoir.

3. Complete the similes.

   a. The infant girl was as lovely as _____.

   b. The boy waved his arms like _____.

   c. The panda's belly was a round as _____.

   d. The mountains were jagged like _____.

48

4. Fill in the blanks to complete the similes.

   a. The _____ was like _____.

   b. The _____ was like _____.

   c. The _____ was as _____ as _____.

   d. The _____ was as _____ as _____.

CREATE NOVEL ARTWORK (Draw someone you admire.)

LESSON 11: "I WANDERED LONELY AS A CLOUD" BY WILLIAM WORDSWORTH (SIMILE)

FEATURED POEM

1. I wandered lonely as a cloud
   That floats on high o'er vales and hills,
When all at once I saw a crowd,
   A host, of golden daffodils;
Beside the lake, beneath the trees,
Fluttering and dancing in the breeze.

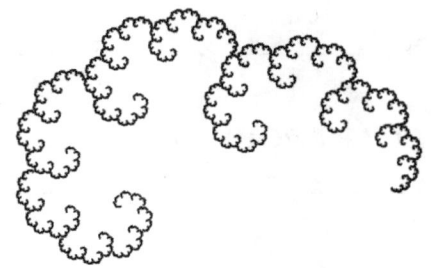

2. Continuous as the stars that shine
   And twinkle on the milky way,
They stretched in never-ending line
   Along the margin of a bay:
Ten thousand saw I at a glance,
Tossing their heads in sprightly dance.

3. The waves beside them danced; but they
   Out-did the sparkling waves in glee:
A poet could not but be gay,
   In such a jocund company:
I gazed—and gazed—but little thought
What wealth the show to me had brought:

4. For oft, when on my couch I lie
   In vacant or in pensive mood,
They flash upon that inward eye
   Which is the bliss of solitude;
And then my heart with pleasure fills,
And dances with the daffodils.

SYNOPSIS

William Wordsworth's poem, "I Wandered Lonely as a Cloud," describes the narrator finding a field of daffodils along a lake shore. At this time, he does not yet realize the worth of this encounter. Long after he's left the scene, when he's lonely or restless, the recollection of the daffodils makes him happy.

RECITE POEM, TITLE, AND POET

Practice reciting the poem, the poem title, and the name of the poet.

NARRATE THE POEM

_____

_____

_____

_____

_____

COMPLETE COPYWORK

I wandered lonely as a cloud
That floats on high o'er vales and hills,
When all at once I saw a crowd,
A host, of golden daffodils;

_____

_____

_____

_____

ELEMENTARY POETRY VOLUME 5: LITERARY DEVICES

COMPLETE DICTATION

_____

_____

_____

_____

_____

DEVICE IDENTIFICATION AND EMPLOYMENT

1. Recognize Use of Similes
   - Recite the sentences.
   - Circle the simile clues in each sentence — "as" or "like."
     a. The boy heard a crackling sound like a campfire.
     b. The villain was as mean as a junkyard dog.
     c. The plan was as diabolical as the devil.
     d. The bone snapped like a twig.
     e. She was as clever as a fox.

2. Identify the Similes and Rhyming Scheme
   a. Circle the similes in the poem excerpt.
   b. Assign letters to the sentences to reveal the rhyming scheme.

	Rhyming Scheme (e.g. A-A-B-B)
I wandered lonely as a cloud	( )
That floats on high o'er vales and hills,	( )
When all at once I saw a crowd,	( )
A host, of golden daffodils;	( )
Beside the lake, beneath the trees,	( )
Fluttering and dancing in the breeze.	( )
Continuous as the stars that shine	( )
And twinkle on the milky way,	( )
They stretched in never-ending line	( )
Along the margin of a bay:	( )
Ten thousand saw I at a glance,	( )
Tossing their heads in sprightly dance.	( )

3. Write a poem of six lines, employing at least one simile (like, as) and the traditional rhyming scheme.

_____ (A)

_____ (B)

_____ (A)

_____ (B)

_____ (A)

_____ (B)

CREATE NOVEL ARTWORK (Sketch a recollection that brings you happiness.)

LESSON 12: "BIRCHES"
BY ROBERT FROST (SIMILE)

FEATURED POEM

When I see birches bend to left and right
Across the lines of straighter darker trees,
I like to think some boy's been swinging them.
But swinging doesn't bend them down to stay
Ice-storms do that. Often you must have seen them
Loaded with ice a sunny winter morning
After a rain. They click upon themselves
As the breeze rises, and turn many-colored
As the stir cracks and crazes their enamel.
Soon the sun's warmth makes them shed crystal shells
Shattering and avalanching on the snow-crust—
Such heaps of broken glass to sweep away
You'd think the inner dome of heaven had fallen.
They are dragged to the withered bracken by the load,
And they seem not to break; though once they are bowed
So low for long, they never right themselves:
You may see their trunks arching in the woods
Years afterwards, trailing their leaves on the ground
Like girls on hands and knees that throw their hair
Before them over their heads to dry in the sun.
But I was going to say when Truth broke in
With all her matter-of-fact about the ice-storm
Now am I free to be poetical
I should prefer to have some boy bend them
As he went out and in to fetch the cows—
Some boy too far from town to learn baseball,
Whose only play was what he found himself,
Summer or winter, and could play alone.
One by one he subdued his father's trees

Birch Tree

Birch Leaf

By riding them down over and over again
Until he took the stiffness out of them,
And not one but hung limp, not one was left
For him to conquer. He learned all there was
To learn about not launching out too soon
And so not carrying the tree away
Clear to the ground. He always kept his poise
To the top branches, climbing carefully
With the same pains you use to fill a cup
Up to the brim, and even above the brim.
Then he flung outward, feet first, with a swish,
Kicking his way down through the air to the ground.
So was I once myself a swinger of birches.
And so I dream of going back to be.
It's when I'm weary of considerations,
And life is too much like a pathless wood
Where your face burns and tickles with the cobwebs
Broken across it, and one eye is weeping
From a twig's having lashed across it open.
I'd like to get away from earth awhile
And then come back to it and begin over.
May no fate willfully misunderstand me
And half grant what I wish and snatch me away
Not to return. Earth's the right place for love:
I don't know where it's likely to go better.
I'd like to go by climbing a birch tree,
And climb black branches up a snow-white trunk
Toward heaven, till the tree could bear no more,
But dipped its top and set me down again.
That would be good both going and coming back.
One could do worse than be a swinger of birches.

Birch Branch

Birch Seed

SYNOPSIS

In Robert Frost's poem, "Birches," the swaying of the birches in the wind reminds the narrator of climbing birch trees during their childhood. The narrator recalls how ice storms may temporarily or even permanently bend the birch trees, but do not break them. The narrator longs to leave earth and to return as a boy again so he can once again be a swinger of birches. The poet uses similes to add to the pleasant impact of the poem.

RECITE POEM, TITLE, AND POET

Practice reciting the poem, the poem title, and the name of the poet.

NARRATE THE POEM

_____

_____

_____

_____

COMPLETE COPYWORK

When I see birches bend to left and right
Across the lines of straighter darker trees,
I like to think some boy's been swinging them.

_____

_____

_____

_____

COMPLETE DICTATION

_____

_____

_____

_____

_____

DEVICE IDENTIFICATION AND EMPLOYMENT

1. Recognize Use of Similes
   - Recite the sentences.
   - Circle the simile clues in each sentence – "as" or "like."
     a. The calm water reflected the trees like a mirror.
     b. He was as big as a giant.
     c. Her lips were as bright as pink rose petals.
     d. Her eyes sparkled like amethyst.
     e. His eyebrows looked like two fuzzy caterpillars.

2. Circle the Alliterative Words
   a. B: When I see birches bend to left and right
   b. CR: As the stir cracks and crazes their enamel.
   c. T: Toward heaven, till the tree could bear no more,
   d. W: One could do worse than be a swinger of birches.

3. Find the Similes
   Study the poem excerpt and circle the similes.

   > You may see their trunks arching in the woods
   > Years afterwards, trailing their leaves on the ground
   > Like girls on hands and knees that throw their hair
   > Before them over their heads to dry in the sun.
   > And life is too much like a pathless wood
   > Where your face burns and tickles with the cobwebs
   > Broken across it, and one eye is weeping
   > From a twig's having lashed across it open.

ELEMENTARY POETRY VOLUME 5: LITERARY DEVICES

4. Write a poem of six lines, employing at least one simile (like, as) and the triplet rhyming scheme.

_____ (A)

_____ (A)

_____ (A)

_____ (B)

_____ (B)

_____ (B)

CREATE NOVEL ARTWORK (Illustrate a happy scene from your childhood.)

PART IV: METAPHOR

INTRODUCTION

Recall that literary devices are defined as "rules of thumb, convention, or structure that are employed in literature and storytelling." The poems of the next four lessons are vessels brimming with metaphors.

1. Rhyming
2. Alliteration
3. Simile
4. **Metaphor**
5. Personification
6. Foreshadowing
7. Allusion
8. Hyperbole
9. Onomatopoeia

Metaphors use a word or phrase to refer to something that they are not to make an implied comparison. Metaphors make comparison like similes, but they do not employ the words "like" or "as" to make the comparison.

Circle the two subjects being compared in each sentence in accordance with the answers in parentheses.

- The immense desk was a field sprouting pencils and papers. (Desk compared to field)
- The cotton candy was a swirling pink cloud. (Cotton candy compared to a cloud)
- The little boy was a pig, rooting through his mashed potatoes with his snout. (Boy compared to pig)
- The sea of wildflowers waved in the breeze. (Wildflowers compared to the sea)
- She was a ray of sunshine, brightening everyone she touched. (Female compared to ray of sunlight)
- His eyes were jagged glass, slicing into everyone around her. (Eyes compared to glass)

The list below presents some commonly used metaphors. Circle the two subjects being compared in each sentence in accordance with the provided answers in parentheses.

- He was a lion on the battlefield. (Man compared to lion)
- She has a heart of gold. (Temperament compared to a golden heart)
- It's raining cats and dogs. (Heavy rain compared to cats and dogs)
- He was a night owl. (Person compared to owl)
- Love is a battlefield. (Love compared to battlefield)
- The room was a sea of fire. (fire compared to the sea)

ELEMENTARY POETRY VOLUME 5: LITERARY DEVICES

LESSON 13: "THE SUN RISING" BY JOHN DONNE (METAPHOR)

FEATURED POEM

1.   Busy old fool, unruly Sun,

        Why dost thou thus,

Through windows, and through curtains call on us?

Must to thy motions lovers' seasons run?

        Saucy pedantic wretch, go chide

        Late school boys and sour prentices,

   Go tell court huntsmen that the king will ride,

   Call country ants to harvest offices,

Love, all alike, no season knows nor clime,

Nor hours, days, months, which are the rags of time.

2.   Thy beams, so reverend and strong

        Why shouldst thou think?

I could eclipse and cloud them with a wink,

But that I would not lose her sight so long;

    If her eyes have not blinded thine,

    Look, and tomorrow late, tell me,

Whether both th' Indias of spice and mine

Be where thou leftst them, or lie here with me.

Ask for those kings whom thou saw'st yesterday,

And thou shalt hear, "All here in one bed lay."

3.   She's all states, and all princes, I,

        Nothing else is.

Princes do but play us; compared to this,

All honor's mimic, all wealth alchemy.

    Thou, Sun, art half as happy as we,

        In that the world's contracted thus.

    Thine age asks ease, and since thy duties be

        To warm the world, that's done in warming us.

Shine here to us, and thou art everywhere;

This bed thy center is, these walls, thy sphere.

SYNOPSIS

In John Donne's "The Sun Rising," the narrator scolds the sun for waking him, for he prefers to remain cocooned with his true love. The narrator refuses to close his eyes to block the sun because he'd lose sight of his true love. The rest of the world does not matter to the narrator, whether it involves king or prince or wealth or expensive spices. All that matters is his true love. The narrator considers their bed the center of his bedroom universe. In this poem, Donne employs a literary device called a metaphor to make comparisons.

RECITE POEM, TITLE, AND POET

Practice reciting the poem, the poem title, and the name of the poet.

NARRATE THE POEM

_____

_____

_____

_____

_____

_____

COMPLETE COPYWORK

Busy old fool, unruly sun,
Why dost thou thus,
Through windows, and through curtains call on us?

_____

_____

_____

_____

COMPLETE DICTATION

_____

_____

_____

_____

DEVICE IDENTIFICATION AND EMPLOYMENT

1. Recite the sentences containing metaphors. Write the two items being compared in the blanks.

    a. Her cheeks were two red cherries. (_____ compared to _____)

    b. His fingers were icicles. (_____ compared to _____)

    c. Little tornado Davy ripped through the toybox. (_____ compared to _____)

    d. The blanket of night smothered the light. (_____ compared to _____)

    e. The kite soared, flapping its wings. (_____ compared to _____)

2. Locate a few examples of alliteration in the poem.

3. Find the Metaphors and Rhyming Scheme
    a. Circle the metaphors in the poem excerpt.
    b. Assign letters to the sentences to reveal the rhyming scheme.

	Rhyming Scheme (e.g. A-A-B-B)
She's all states, and all princes, I,	( )
Nothing else is.	( )
Princes do but play us; compared to this,	( )
All honor's mimic, all wealth alchemy.	( )
Thou, sun, art half as happy as we,	( )
In that the world's contracted thus.	( )
Thine age asks ease, and since thy duties be	( )
To warm the world, that's done in warming us.	( )
Shine here to us, and thou art everywhere;	( )
This bed thy center is, these walls, thy sphere.	( )

4. Complete the metaphors.

   a. The man was a _____.

   b. The girl is a _____.

   c. The wolf is a _____.

   d. The baby's toes were _____.

CREATE NOVEL ARTWORK (Draw something you treasure like the narrator cherishes his beloved.)

LESSON 14: "SHALL I COMPARE THEE?" BY WILLIAM SHAKESPEARE (METAPHOR)

FEATURED POEM

POEM	TRANSLATION
Shall I compare thee to a summer's day?	Shall I compare you to a summer's day?
Thou art more lovely and more temperate.	You are more beautiful and fair than a summer's day.
Rough winds do shake the darling buds of May,	Winds shake the buds of leaves and flowers in May,
And summer's lease hath all too short a date.	And summer ends too quickly.
Sometime too hot the eye of heaven shines,	The sun is sometimes too hot,
And often is his gold complexion dimmed;	Clouds often cover and dim the sun;
And every fair from fair sometime declines,	Everything beautiful fades,
By chance, or nature's changing course, untrimmed;	Either from bad luck or the natural passage of time;
But thy eternal summer shall not fade,	But your youthful beauty will never fade,
Nor lose possession of that fair thou ow'st,	You will never lose the loveliness you own,
Nor shall death brag thou wand'rest in his shade,	Death will not get you,
When in eternal lines to Time thou grow'st.	Because you will live forever in my poem.
So long as men can breathe, or eyes can see,	As long as people can live and see,
So long lives this, and this gives life to thee.	My poem will keep you alive.

SYNOPSIS

William Shakespeare's "Shall I Compare Thee to a Summer's Day," is an extended metaphor, comparing the narrator's true love to a summer's day and finding the lovely day lacking. The narrator consoles his beloved that she will remain alive and young and beautiful forever through his poem. Keep in mind that as you read the poem, you personally are helping the narrator keep the memory of his beloved alive.

RECITE POEM, TITLE, AND POET

Practice reciting the poem, the poem title, and the name of the poet.

NARRATE THE POEM

_____

_____

_____

_____

COMPLETE COPYWORK

Shall I compare thee to a summer's day?
Thou art more lovely and more temperate.
Rough winds do shake the darling buds of May,

_____

_____

_____

_____

COMPLETE DICTATION

_____

_____

_____

_____

DEVICE IDENTIFICATION AND EMPLOYMENT

1. Recite the sentences containing metaphors. Write the two items being compared in the blanks.

    a. The museum curator is an old dinosaur. (_____ compared to _____)

    b. Sally is a fraidy cat. (_____ compared to _____)

    c. Her bedroom was a disaster zone. (_____ compared to _____)

    d. The vampire grinned, revealing bone daggers. (_____ compared to _____)

    e. His garden was paradise on earth. (_____ compared to _____)

2. Identify the Metaphors and Rhyming Words
    a. Circle the metaphors in the poem excerpt.
    b. Assign letters to the sentences to reveal the rhyming scheme.

	Rhyming Scheme (e.g. A-A-B-B)
Sometime too hot the eye of heaven shines,	( )
And often is his gold complexion dimmed;	( )
And every fair from fair sometime declines,	( )
By chance, or nature's changing course, untrimmed;	( )
But thy eternal summer shall not fade,	( )
Nor lose possession of that fair thou ow'st,	( )
Nor shall death brag thou wand'rest in his shade,	( )
When in eternal lines to Time thou grow'st.	( )

3. Fill in the blanks to complete the metaphors.

   a. The _____ was a _____.

   b. The _____ was a _____.

   c. The _____ is a _____.

   d. The _____ is a _____.

CREATE NOVEL ARTWORK (Illustrate something you find beautiful.)

LESSON 15: "WHEN I HAVE FEARS" BY JOHN KEATS (METAPHOR)

FEATURED POEM

POEM	TRANSLATION
When I have fears that I may cease to be	When I fear dying
Before my pen has gleaned my teeming brain,	Before I've written everything I want to write about
Before high-pilèd books, in charactery,	Before I've written a big stack of books
Hold like rich garners the full ripened grain;	The books are a granary holding my words of ripe grain
When I behold, upon the night's starred face,	When I look at the starry night sky
Huge cloudy symbols of a high romance,	I see foretellings of romance in the clouds
And think that I may never live to trace	However, I fear I might not live long enough
Their shadows with the magic hand of chance;	To find that fated love
And when I feel, fair creature of an hour,	I worry, my beautiful and short-lived, mortal true love
That I shall never look upon thee more,	That I will never see you
Never have relish in the faery power	But I've never really liked mystical,
Of unreflecting love—then on the shore	All-consuming love
Of the wide world I stand alone, and think	I stand alone on the shore of the world, thinking
Till love and fame to nothingness do sink.	Until love and fame no longer matter to me.

SYNOPSIS

In John Keats' stark and ponderous poem, "When I have Fears," the narrator discusses his fears of not fully realizing his potential in life. He worries he will not write enough books. He worries he won't meet his fated true love. But as he ponders the universe, he realizes that earthly fame and love may ultimately be meaningless.

RECITE POEM, TITLE, AND POET

Practice reciting the poem, the poem title, and the name of the poet.

NARRATE THE POEM

_____

_____

_____

_____

COMPLETE COPYWORK

When I have fears that I may cease to be
Before my pen has gleaned my teeming brain,
Before high-pilèd books, in charactery,
Hold like rich garners the full ripened grain;

_____

_____

_____

_____

COMPLETE DICTATION

_____

_____

_____

_____

DEVICE IDENTIFICATION AND EMPLOYMENT

1. Recite the sentences containing metaphors. Write the two items being compared in the blanks.

    a. The old firecracker danced a spirited jig. (_____ compared to _____)

    b. The ballroom was a fairyland. (_____ compared to _____)

    c. The oven in the sky baked us with its rays. (_____ compared to _____)

    d. The truck was a growling monster. (_____ compared to _____)

    e. The child was a whirling dervish. (_____ compared to _____)

2. Review the poem and identify a few examples of alliteration.

3. Identify the Metaphors and Rhyming Words
    a. Circle the metaphors in the poem excerpt.
    b. Assign letters to the sentences to reveal the rhyming scheme.

	Rhyming Scheme (e.g. A-A-B-B)
When I have fears that I may cease to be	( )
Before my pen has gleaned my teeming brain,	( )
Before high-pilèd books, in charactery,	( )
Hold like rich garners the full ripened grain;	( )
When I behold, upon the night's starred face,	( )
Huge cloudy symbols of a high romance,	( )
And think that I may never live to trace	( )
Their shadows with the magic hand of chance;	( )

4. Write a poem of six lines, employing at least one metaphor and the traditional rhyming scheme.

_____ (A)

_____ (B)

_____ (A)

_____ (B)

_____ (A)

_____ (B)

CREATE NOVEL ARTWORK (Portray something you fear.)

LESSON 16: "SYMPATHY"
BY PAUL LAURENCE DUNBAR (METAPHOR)

FEATURED POEM

I know what the caged bird feels, alas!

    When the sun is bright on the upland slopes;

When the wind stirs soft through the springing grass,

And the river flows like a stream of glass;

    When the first bird sings and the first bud opes,

And the faint perfume from its chalice steals—

I know what the caged bird feels!

I know why the caged bird beats his wing

    Till its blood is red on the cruel bars;

For he must fly back to his perch and cling

When he fain would be on the bough a-swing;

    And a pain still throbs in the old, old scars

And they pulse again with a keener sting—

I know why he beats his wing!

I know why the caged bird sings, ah me,

    When his wing is bruised and his bosom sore,—

When he beats his bars and he would be free;

It is not a carol of joy or glee,

    But a prayer that he sends from his heart's deep core,

But a plea, that upward to Heaven he flings—

I know why the caged bird sings!

SYNOPSIS

Paul Laurence Dunbar's heart-wrenching poem, "Sympathy," is an extended metaphor, comparing oppressed people (e.g. minorities in an oppressive society) to a bird trapped in a cage. The bird longs for the beautiful breezes and sunlight of freedom so keenly, it bloodies its beating wings while trying to escape the cage. The bird sings not with happiness, but to pray to heaven for mercy.

RECITE POEM, TITLE, AND POET

Practice reciting the poem, the poem title, and the name of the poet.

NARRATE THE POEM

_____

_____

_____

_____

_____

COMPLETE COPYWORK

I know why the caged bird sings, ah me,
When his wing is bruised and his bosom sore,—
When he beats his bars and he would be free;

_____

_____

_____

_____

COMPLETE DICTATION

_____

_____

_____

_____

DEVICE IDENTIFICATION AND EMPLOYMENT

1. Recite the sentences containing metaphors. Write the two items being compared in the blanks.

    a. Her fingernails were sharpened scissors. (_____ compared to _____)

    b. His nose was a sharp-peaked mountain. (_____ compared to _____)

    c. The mower cut the jungle ensnaring the backyard. (_____ compared to _____)

    d. The girl was a princess in her costume. (_____ compared to _____)

    e. Her runny nose was a faucet. (_____ compared to _____)

2. Find a few examples of alliteration in the poem.

3. Find any similes in the poem and name the pairs of elements compared.

4. Identify the Metaphors and Rhyming Words
    a. Circle the metaphors in the poem excerpt.
    b. Assign letters to the sentences to reveal the rhyming scheme.

	Rhyming Scheme (e.g. A-A-B-B)
I know why the caged bird beats his wing	( )
Till its blood is red on the cruel bars;	( )
For he must fly back to his perch and cling	( )
When he fain would be on the bough a-swing;	( )
And a pain still throbs in the old, old scars	( )
And they pulse again with a keener sting—	( )
I know why he beats his wing!	( )

5. Write a poem of six lines, employing at least one metaphor and the couplet rhyming scheme.

_____ (A)

_____ (A)

_____ (B)

_____ (B)

_____ (C)

_____ (C)

CREATE NOVEL ARTWORK (Illustrate your ideas on captivity and freedom.)

PART V: PERSONIFICATION

INTRODUCTION

Recall that literary devices are defined as "rules of thumb, convention, or structure that are employed in literature and storytelling." The next four professorial lessons don their reading glasses as they lecture the reader on the use of personification in poetry.

1. Rhyming
2. Alliteration
3. Simile
4. Metaphor
5. **Personification**
6. Foreshadowing
7. Allusion
8. Hyperbole
9. Onomatopoeia

Personification is a literary device in which an object or an idea is given human qualities. For example:

Personification Example	Explanation
The bee scolded the little boy who neared its hive.	The bee is personified via the human action of scolding.
The stone merrily skipped down the steep slope.	The stone is personified via the human action of skipping and the human emotion of merriment.
The horse said hello to the little girl.	The horse is personified via the human action of saying hello.
The moon beamed down at the boy with love.	The moon is personified with the human action of beaming (smiling).
The rotten smell of garbage smacked me over the head.	The scent is personified with the human action of striking someone.
The pants on the clothes line danced a sprightly jig in the wind.	The pants are personified with the human action of dancing a jig.

LESSON 17: "STOPPING BY WOODS ON A SNOWY EVENING" BY ROBERT FROST (PERSONIFICATION)

FEATURED POEM

Whose woods these are I think I know.

His house is in the village though;

He will not see me stopping here

To watch his woods fill up with snow.

My little horse must think it queer

To stop without a farmhouse near

Between the woods and frozen lake

The darkest evening of the year.

He gives his harness bells a shake

To ask if there is some mistake.

The only other sound's the sweep

Of easy wind and downy flake.

The woods are lovely, dark and deep,

But I have promises to keep,

And miles to go before I sleep,

And miles to go before I sleep.

SYNOPSIS

"Stopping by Woods on a Snowy Evening" by Robert Frost personifies a horse. The horse thinks things are strange and shakes its harness to ask whether a mistake has been made when the narrator stops in the middle of the dark woods. The narrator thinks he knows who owns the property he's stopped upon. However, the owner lives in town and will never know he stopped there. The narrator knows he must get going. He has miles to go before he reaches his destination. It remains an intriguing mystery as to why the narrator stopped at that particular place in the woods.

RECITE POEM, TITLE, AND POET

Practice reciting the poem, the poem title, and the name of the poet.

NARRATE THE POEM

_____

_____

_____

_____

COMPLETE COPYWORK

My little horse must think it queer
To stop without a farmhouse near
Between the woods and frozen lake
The darkest evening of the year.

_____

_____

_____

_____

ELEMENTARY POETRY VOLUME 5: LITERARY DEVICES

COMPLETE DICTATION

_____

_____

_____

_____

DEVICE IDENTIFICATION AND EMPLOYMENT

1. Recite the examples and identify the object being personified.

   a. The leaf danced across the yard. (_____ is personified)

   b. The sun peeped out through the clouds. (_____ is personified)

   c. The mower muttered in disgust when I tried to start it. (_____ is personified)

   d. The scent of apple pie crooked its finger, beckoning me. (_____ is personified)

   e. The tornado siren wailed through the night. (_____ is personified)

2. Find a few examples of alliteration in the poem.

3. Identify the Metaphors and Rhyming Words
   a. Circle the instances of personification in the poem excerpt.
   b. Assign letters to the sentences to reveal the rhyming scheme.

	Rhyming Scheme (e.g. A-A-B-B)
My little horse must think it queer	( )
To stop without a farmhouse near	( )
Between the woods and frozen lake	( )
The darkest evening of the year.	( )
He gives his harness bells a shake	( )
To ask if there is some mistake.	( )
The only other sound's the sweep	( )
Of easy wind and downy flake.	( )

4. Complete the sentences to personify each subject.

   a. The dog _____.

   b. The clock _____.

   c. The wolf _____.

   d. The house _____.

CREATE NOVEL ARTWORK (Draw a personified horse.)

LESSON 18: "SHE SWEEPS WITH MANY-COLORED BROOMS" BY EMILY DICKINSON (PERSONIFICATION)

FEATURED POEM

She sweeps with many-colored brooms,

And leaves the shreds behind;

Oh, housewife in the evening west,

Come back, and dust the pond!

You dropped a purple ravelling in,

You dropped an amber thread;

And now you've littered all the East

With duds of emerald!

And still she plies her spotted brooms,

And still the aprons fly,

Till brooms fade softly into stars—

And then I come away.

SYNOPSIS

Emily Dickinson's charming "She Sweeps with Many-Colored Brooms," personifies the sun. Dickinson compares the setting sun with a housewife who sweeps her house at the end of the day. The rays of light are compared to a broom that leaves behind fragments, or the lingering colors of the sunset. The housewife's white apron represents the flying clouds. The broom and its colorful remnants slowly fade away into stars as night approaches.

RECITE POEM, TITLE, AND POET

Practice reciting the poem, the poem title, and the name of the poet.

NARRATE THE POEM

_____

_____

_____

_____

COMPLETE COPYWORK

She sweeps with many-colored brooms,
And leaves the shreds behind;
Oh, housewife in the evening west,
Come back, and dust the pond!

_____

_____

_____

_____

COMPLETE DICTATION

_____

_____

_____

_____

DEVICE IDENTIFICATION AND EMPLOYMENT

1. Recite the examples and identify the object being personified.

    a. The ocean waved a frothy farewell. (_____ is personified)

    b. The fire hissed angrily as I doused it with water. (_____ is personified)

    c. The bird sang, imploring me to come outside. (_____ is personified)

    d. The parched earth drank up the rain. (_____ is personified)

    e. The angry welt across her arm turned purple. (_____ is personified)

2. Study the poem and circle any instances of personification.

    She sweeps with many-colored brooms,
    And leaves the shreds behind;
    Oh, housewife in the evening west,
    Come back, and dust the pond!

    You dropped a purple ravelling in,
    You dropped an amber thread;
    And now you've littered all the East
    With duds of emerald!

    And still she plies her spotted brooms,
    And still the aprons fly,
    Till brooms fade softly into stars—
    And then I come away.

3. Complete the sentences to personify each subject.

   a. The broom _____.

   b. The dress _____.

   c. The old groundhog _____.

   d. The star _____.

CREATE NOVEL ARTWORK (Illustrate a personified sun.)

LESSON 19: "MOWING"
BY ROBERT FROST (PERSONIFICATION)

FEATURED POEM

There was never a sound beside the wood but one,
And that was my long scythe whispering to the ground.
What was it it whispered? I knew not well myself;
Perhaps it was something about the heat of the sun,
Something, perhaps, about the lack of sound—
And that was why it whispered and did not speak.
It was no dream of the gift of idle hours,
Or easy gold at the hand of fay or elf:
Anything more than the truth would have seemed too weak
To the earnest love that laid the swale in rows,
Not without feeble-pointed spikes of flowers
Pale orchises, and scared a bright green snake.
The fact is the sweetest dream that labor knows.
My long scythe whispered and left the hay to make.

SYNOPSIS

In Robert Frost's "Mowing," the narrator cuts hay and imagines their scythe is whispering secret messages to the ground. They ponder what the scythe is saying - perhaps something about the hot sun or the quiet. They don't think the scythe dreams of lazing about or easy riches. Rather, the narrator believes accomplishing simple work is enough for the scythe, whether by cutting rows of hay or scaring green snakes.

RECITE POEM, TITLE, AND POET

Practice reciting the poem, the poem title, and the name of the poet.

NARRATE THE POEM

_____

_____

_____

_____

COMPLETE COPYWORK

There was never a sound beside the wood but one,
And that was my long scythe whispering to the ground.
What was it it whispered? I knew not well myself;

_____

_____

_____

_____

COMPLETE DICTATION

_____

_____

_____

_____

DEVICE IDENTIFICATION AND EMPLOYMENT

1. Recite the examples and identify the object being personified.
   a. The sullen leaf refused to float down the gutter. (_____ is personified)
   b. The daisy bobbed its head in time to the bird song. (_____ is personified)
   c. The snake hissed menacing threats to the small boy. (_____ is personified)
   d. The diamond ring flashed, mocking in its brilliance. (_____ is personified)
   e. The roof groaned it would succumb to the hurricane. (_____ is personified)

2. Identify the Personification Instances and Rhyming Words
   a. Circle the instances of personification in the poem excerpt.
   b. Assign letters to the sentences to reveal the rhyming scheme.

	Rhyming Scheme (e.g. A-A-B-B)
There was never a sound beside the wood but one,	( )
And that was my long scythe whispering to the ground.	( )
What was it it whispered? I know not well myself;	( )
Perhaps it was something about the heat of the sun,	( )
Something perhaps, about the lack of sound—	( )
And that was why it whispered and did not speak.	( )
It was not dream of the gift of idle hours,	( )
Or easy gold at the hand of fay or elf:	( )
Anything more than the truth would have seemed too weak	( )
To the earnest love that laid the swale in rows,	( )
Not without feeble-pointed spikes of flowers	( )
(Pale orchises), and scared a bright green snake.	( )
The fact is the sweetest dream that labor knows.	( )
My long scythe whispered and left the hay to make.	( )

3. Write a poem of six lines, employing personification at least once and the designated rhyming scheme.

_____ (A)

_____ (B)

_____ (B)

_____ (A)

_____ (C)

_____ (C)

CREATE NOVEL ARTWORK (Sketch a personified scythe.)

ELEMENTARY POETRY VOLUME 5: LITERARY DEVICES

LESSON 20: "THE RAILWAY TRAIN"
BY EMILY DICKINSON (PERSONIFICATION)

FEATURED POEM

I like to see it lap the miles,
And lick the valleys up,
And stop to feed itself at tanks;
And then, prodigious, step

Around a pile of mountains,
And, supercilious, peer
In shanties, by the sides of roads;
And then a quarry pare

To fit its sides, and crawl between,
Complaining all the while
In horrid, hooting stanza;
Then chase itself downhill

And neigh like Boanerges;
Then, punctual as a star,
Stop--docile and omnipotent--
At its own stable door.

SYNOPSIS

Emily Dickinson's "The Railway Train" personifies a traveling train. The poem can also be seen as an extended metaphor, comparing the train to an animal. The animalistic train laps up miles, licks up valleys, feeds at fuel tanks, crawls, and neighs.

RECITE POEM, TITLE, AND POET

Practice reciting the poem, the poem title, and the name of the poet.

NARRATE THE POEM

_____

_____

_____

_____

_____

COMPLETE COPYWORK

I like to see it lap the miles,
And lick the valleys up,
And stop to feed itself at tanks;
And then, prodigious, step

_____

_____

_____

_____

ELEMENTARY POETRY VOLUME 5: LITERARY DEVICES

COMPLETE DICTATION

_____

_____

_____

_____

DEVICE IDENTIFICATION AND EMPLOYMENT

1. Recite the examples and identify the object being personified.
    a. The cockroach sauntered across the table. (_____ is personified)
    b. The star winked at me. (_____ is personified)
    c. I broke the pencil's backbone. (_____ is personified)
    d. The big dog laughed at the little dog. (_____ is personified)
    e. The llama stuck its nose in the air and sashayed off. (_____ is personified)

2. Find any similes in the poem and name the pairs of elements compared.

3. Study the poem and circle any instances of personification.

   I like to see it lap the miles,
   And lick the valleys up,
   And stop to feed itself at tanks;
   And then, prodigious, step

   Around a pile of mountains,
   And, supercilious, peer
   In shanties, by the sides of roads;
   And then a quarry pare

   To fit its sides, and crawl between,
   Complaining all the while
   In horrid, hooting stanza;
   Then chase itself downhill.

4. Write a poem of six lines, employing personification at least once and the designated rhyming scheme.

_____ (A)

_____ (A)

_____ (B)

_____ (C)

_____ (C)

_____ (B)

CREATE NOVEL ARTWORK (Draw a personified object of your choice.)

PART VI: FORESHADOWING

INTRODUCTION

Recall that literary devices are defined as "rules of thumb, convention, or structure that are employed in literature and storytelling." The next four lessons introduce foreshadowing in poetry, portending future literary successes for the studious reader.

1. Rhyming
2. Alliteration
3. Simile
4. Metaphor
5. Personification
6. **Foreshadowing**
7. Allusion
8. Hyperbole
9. Onomatopoeia

Foreshadowing is a literary device whereby an author drops hints or symbolic representations of plot developments to come later in the story. For example:

Foreshadowing Example	Explanation
Ominous music emanated from the open door of the dilapidated house. "Don't come inside, you'd better hide," crooned the singer.	The song lyrics foreshadow trouble if anyone enters the house.
Aunt Milly stumbled, clutching her knee. "My arthritis flares whenever there's a storm," she said. "But I've never felt a pain as bad as this one."	Aunt Milly's extreme knee pain foreshadows a record-setting storm in the near future.
As the girl walked the dog down the dark, wooded path, the hair on the back of the dog's neck raised and he growled.	The dog's hair standing up and his growing foreshadow danger approaching.
"If I won the lottery, I'd buy my mom a new wheelchair," the boy said. "But miracles don't happen to people like us." The richly dressed stranger smiled at the boy. "Don't lose hope. Miracles happen every day to all types of people."	The stranger's words foreshadow that he may help the boy's mother in the future.
The little girl peered into the cave, curiosity lighting up her face. "Never go into the cave," the girl's mother warned.	The excerpt foreshadows that the girl will go into the cave and encounter danger.
The old soothsayer dropped the chicken bones, which clattered onto the table and formed a skull and crossbones shape. "The pirates are blowing this way," she hissed. "And death is coming with them."	The chicken bones symbolize and foreshadow the arrival of pirates, conflict, and death.

LESSON 21: "SPRING RAIN"
BY SARA TEASDALE (FORESHADOWING)

FEATURED POEM

I thought I had forgotten,
But it all came back again
Tonight with the first spring thunder
In a rush of rain.

I remembered a darkened doorway
Where we stood while the storm swept by,
Thunder gripping the earth
And lightning scrawled on the sky.

The passing motor busses swayed,
For the street was a river of rain,
Lashed into little golden waves
In the lamp light's stain.

With the wild spring rain and thunder
My heart was wild and gay;
Your eyes said more to me that night
Than your lips would ever say...

I thought I had forgotten,
But it all came back again
Tonight with the first spring thunder
In a rush of rain.

SYNOPSIS

Sara Teasdale's "Spring Rain" uses both flashbacks and foreshadowing for effect. A spring thunderstorm causes the narrator to flash back to a time when she waited out a storm in a doorway with another person. Little details, such as the passing busses and the light shining on the water, have stuck in the narrator's memory. The narrator gazed into the other person's eyes as her heart pounded, hinting at romance. The two exchange looks saying more than any of their future conversations, foreshadowing perhaps they would soon part ways.

RECITE POEM, TITLE, AND POET

Practice reciting the poem, the poem title, and the name of the poet.

NARRATE THE POEM

_____

_____

_____

_____

COMPLETE COPYWORK

I thought I had forgotten,
But it all came back again
Tonight with the first spring thunder
In a rush of rain.

_____

_____

_____

COMPLETE DICTATION

_____

_____

_____

_____

DEVICE IDENTIFICATION AND EMPLOYMENT

1. Recite the examples and write your prediction of the future event being foreshadowed.
    a. The pack of children fled the furious man. "Don't fall behind," Sarah warned little Timmy.

    _____

    "I'll easily carry you," Mark boasted to Sally, flexing his biceps. "Don't bet on it," Sally replied.

    _____

    b. "Call if you need me," Peter's mother said. Peter waved, not realizing he'd forgotten his phone.

    _____

    c. Every time the boy passed the woman's perfectly groomed house, he shivered.

    _____

    d. Larry's father ended the call. "Better hope you never meet your Uncle Jim," he said to Larry.

    _____

2. Find a few examples of alliteration in the poem.

3. Identify the Devices
    a. Circle the instances of foreshadowing in the poem excerpt.
    b. Assign letters to the sentences to reveal the rhyming scheme.

	Rhyming Scheme (e.g. A-A-B-B)
With the wild spring rain and thunder	( )
My heart was wild and gay;	( )
Your eyes said more to me that night	( )
Than your lips would ever say...	( )

4. Complete the sentences to foreshadow or hint something to come in the future.

   a. If only I had known _____
   _____.

   b. "Jimmy, be sure to _____," said my mother.

   c. A crystal ball might have told me _____
   _____.

   d. "Don't forget your _____," my teacher warned.

CREATE NOVEL ARTWORK (Draw something you once forgot and then remembered.)

LESSON 22: "I HAVE A RENDEZVOUS WITH DEATH" BY ALAN SEEGER (FORESHADOWING)

FEATURED POEM

I have a rendezvous with Death

At some disputed barricade,

When Spring comes back with rustling shade

And apple-blossoms fill the air—

I have a rendezvous with Death

When Spring brings back blue days and fair.

It may be he shall take my hand

And lead me into his dark land

And close my eyes and quench my breath—

It may be I shall pass him still.

I have a rendezvous with Death

On some scarred slope of battered hill,

When Spring comes round again this year

And the first meadow-flowers appear.

God knows 'twere better to be deep

Pillowed in silk and scented down,

Where Love throbs out in blissful sleep,

Pulse nigh to pulse, and breath to breath,

Where hushed awakenings are dear...

But I've a rendezvous with Death

At midnight in some flaming town,

When Spring trips north again this year,

And I to my pledged word am true,

I shall not fail that rendezvous.

SYNOPSIS

Moved by idealism, American Alan Seeger volunteered to fight in World War I for the Foreign Legion of France. America had not yet entered the war. Seeger's poem, "I Have a Rendezvous with Death," foreshadows his death in battle. He imagines dying during the following spring on a battle-scarred hill in a burning town at midnight. Seeger's predictions partly came true. He died at the young age of 28 on the 4th of July while fighting in World War I. As Seeger was dying, others reported that he cheered on his fellow soldiers to the very end.

RECITE POEM, TITLE, AND POET

Practice reciting the poem, the poem title, and the name of the poet.

NARRATE THE POEM

_____

_____

_____

_____

COMPLETE COPYWORK

When Spring comes back with rustling shade
And apple-blossoms fill the air—
I have a rendezvous with Death

_____

_____

_____

COMPLETE DICTATION

_____

_____

_____

DEVICE IDENTIFICATION AND EMPLOYMENT

1. Recite the examples and write your prediction of the future event being foreshadowed.
    a. The rickety house leaned precariously. One strong push could collapse the whole thing.
    _____

    b. The red-faced man struggled to climb the hill. "I gotta bad heart," he said to me.
    _____

    c. "Wear your helmet," said Larry's mother. Larry pretended not to hear her as he rode away.
    _____

    d. As the woman in black approached, goosebumps broke out over her skin.
    _____

    e. The town bell clanged. Ben thought it was ringing in the hour, but the bell didn't stop at six.
    _____

2. Find a few examples of alliteration in the poem.
3. Identify the Poetic Devices
    a. Circle the instances of foreshadowing in the poem excerpt.
    b. Assign letters to the sentences to reveal the rhyming scheme.

	Rhyming Scheme (e.g. A-A-B-B)
It may be he shall take my hand	( )
And lead me into his dark land	( )
And close my eyes and quench my breath—	( )
It may be I shall pass him still.	( )
I have a rendezvous with Death	( )
On some scarred slope of battered hill.	( )

4. Complete the sentences to foreshadow or hint at something to come in the future.

   a. Little did I know at the time, _____
   _____.

   b. My future might have been very different if I hadn't _____
   _____.

   c. "If you let me borrow _____
   _____ I promise I won't break it," my sister said.

   d. "If I had just remembered to _____
   _____ things would have turned out differently.

CREATE NOVEL ARTWORK (Draw something that foreshadows good luck in the future.)

LESSON 23: "THE TWINS"
BY HENRY SAMBROOKE LEIGH (FORESHADOWING)

FEATURED POEM

1. In form and feature, face and limb,
I grew so like my brother,
That folks got taking me for him,
And each for one another.
It puzzled all our kith and kin,
It reached a fearful pitch;
For one of us was born a twin,
Yet not a soul knew which.

2. One day, to make the matter worse,
Before our names were fixed,
As we were being washed by nurse,
We got completely mixed;
And thus, you see, by fate's decree,
Or rather nurse's whim,
My brother John got christened me,
And I got christened him.

3. This fatal likeness even dogged
My footsteps when at school,
And I was always getting flogged,
For John turned out a fool.
I put this question, fruitlessly,
To everyone I knew,
"What would you do, if you were me,
To prove that you were you?"

4. Our close resemblance turned the tide
Of my domestic life,
For somehow, my intended bride
Became my brother's wife.
In fact, year after year the same
Absurd mistakes went on,
And when I died, the neighbors came
And buried brother John.

SYNOPSIS

In Henry Sambrooke Leigh's "The Twins," the narrator is mistaken for his identical twin, John, throughout his life. This confusion leads to negative and absurd consequences including being punished for his brother's misdeeds, his brother marrying the narrator's intended bride, and his brother being buried when the narrator dies. In the poem, phrases such as "It reached a fearful pitch" foreshadow the trouble the narrator and his brother will suffer from the twin-related mix-ups.

RECITE POEM, TITLE, AND POET

Practice reciting the poem, the poem title, and the name of the poet.

NARRATE THE POEM

_____

_____

_____

_____

COMPLETE COPYWORK

In form and feature, face and limb,
I grew so like my brother,
That folks got taking me for him,
And each for one another.

_____

_____

_____

_____

COMPLETE DICTATION

_____

_____

_____

_____

DEVICE IDENTIFICATION AND EMPLOYMENT

1. Recite the examples and write your prediction of the future event being foreshadowed.
    a. "Do you smell that?" Timmy asked. "It smells like something burning."
    _____

    b. The phone rang again and again, but each time Suzy answered, no one was on the other line.
    _____

    c. The town's siren wailed, and all of the townsfolk fled to their basements.
    _____

    d. A foreboding chill creeped along my spine as I entered the blackness of the haunted house.
    _____

    e. "One day, your heroic acts will save many lives and gain you fame," said the palm reader.
    _____

2. Find a few examples of alliteration in the poem.

3. Identify the Poetic Devices
    a. Circle the instances of foreshadowing in the poem excerpt.
    b. Assign letters to the sentences to reveal the rhyming scheme.

	Rhyming Scheme (e.g. A-A-B-B)
I grew so like my brother,	( )
That folks got taking me for him,	( )
And each for one another.	( )
It puzzled all our kith and kin,	( )
It reached a fearful pitch;	( )
For one of us was born a twin,	( )
Yet not a soul knew which.	( )

4. Write a poem of six lines, employing foreshadowing at least once and the designated rhyming scheme.

_____ (A)

_____ (B)

_____ (C)

_____ (C)

_____ (B)

_____ (A)

CREATE NOVEL ARTWORK (Draw something that foreshadows an ominous future event.)

LESSON 24: "JABBERWOCKY" BY LEWIS CARROLL (FORESHADOWING)

FEATURED POEM

POEM	TRANSLATION
'Twas brillig, and the slithy toves	It was 4PM, time for cooking dinner, the slimy and lithe
Did gyre and gimble in the wabe;	badger/lizard/corkscrew creatures spun and made holes in the grass.
All mimsy were the borogoves,	The miserable/flimsy birds
And the mome raths outgrabe.	and green pigs bellowed/whistled/sneezed.
"Beware the Jabberwock, my son	Watch out for the Jabberwock son!
The jaws that bite, the claws that catch!	He bites and claws!
Beware the Jubjub bird, and shun	Watch out for the Jubjub bird, and avoid
The frumious Bandersnatch!"	the fuming/furious Bandersnatch (snapping creature that can extend its neck).
He took his vorpal sword in hand;	The son grabs his sword
Long time the manxome foe he sought—	and searches for his enemy for a long time.
So rested he by the Tumtum tree,	He stops to rest by a Tumtum tree
And stood awhile in thought.	And thinks for a bit.
And, as in uffish thought he stood,	As he's thinking and standing,
The Jabberwock, with eyes of flame,	The fiery-eyed Jabberwock,
Came whiffling through the tulgey wood,	Comes wheezing/sniffling through the woods
And burbled as it came!	and makes a bubbling sound.
One, two! One, two! And through and through	The son hits the Jabberwock four times, decapitating it.
The vorpal blade went snicker-snack!	The blade making a snicker-snack sound.
He left it dead, and with its head	The son leaves the Jabberwock dead, and takes its head
He went galumphing back.	and goes trotting/galloping back.
"And hast thou slain the Jabberwock?	Dad asks if his son has really killed the Jabberwock.
Come to my arms, my beamish boy!	Proud dad gives his son a hug.
O frabjous day! Callooh! Callay!"	Dad says, "What a fair, fabulous, and joyous day! Hooray!"
He chortled in his joy.	Dad chuckles with joy.
'Twas brillig, and the slithy toves	It was 4PM, time for cooking dinner, the slimy and lithe
Did gyre and gimble in the wabe;	badger/lizard/corkscrew creatures spun and made holes in the grass.
All mimsy were the borogoves,	The miserable/flimsy birds
And the mome raths outgrabe.	and green pigs bellowed/whistled/sneezed.

SYNOPSIS

Don't worry if you don't recognize all of the words in Lewis Carroll's nonsense poem, "Jabberwocky." Many of the words are made up (see the translation). In the poem, a father warns his son about the fiery-eyed, clawing, biting Jabberwock. The son ignores his father's advice, grabs his sword, and ventures out. After the son kills the Jabberwock, he brings the head back to his father. His father is very proud, and all returns to normal. With the father's warning, the poem employs foreshadowing to hint at the upcoming battle.

RECITE POEM, TITLE, AND POET

Practice reciting the poem, the poem title, and the name of the poet.

NARRATE THE POEM

_____

_____

_____

_____

COMPLETE COPYWORK

"Beware the Jabberwock, my son
The jaws that bite, the claws that catch!

_____

_____

_____

COMPLETE DICTATION

_____

_____

_____

DEVICE IDENTIFICATION AND EMPLOYMENT

1. Recite the examples and write your prediction of the future event being foreshadowed.

    a. As Barry worried about his sick father, the sun broke through the clouds, illuminating Barry.

    _____

    b. A rainbow sparkled over the outdoor graduation ceremony as the valedictorian gave her speech.

    _____

    c. While David studied for his upcoming spelling test, he spotted a four-leaf clover.

    _____

    d. Painful headaches began plaguing Annie. They grew so bad, one day, she couldn't get out of bed.

    _____

2. Find a few examples of alliteration in the poem.

3. Identify the Poetic Devices
    a. Circle the instances of foreshadowing in the poem excerpt.
    b. Assign letters to the sentences to reveal the rhyming scheme.

	Rhyming Scheme (e.g. A-A-B-B)
"Beware the Jabberwock, my son	( )
The jaws that bite, the claws that catch!	( )
Beware the Jubjub bird, and shun	( )
The frumious Bandersnatch!"	( )

    Do the four lines of the poem follow a traditional (ABAB), couplet (AABB), enclosed (ABBA), or triplet (AAABBB) rhyming scheme?

    _____

ELEMENTARY POETRY VOLUME 5: LITERARY DEVICES

4. Write a poem of six lines, employing foreshadowing at least once and the designated rhyming scheme.

_____ (A)

_____ (B)

_____ (C)

_____ (B)

_____ (C)

_____ (A)

CREATE NOVEL ARTWORK (Draw something that foreshadows a stranger coming to town.)

PART VII: ALLUSION

INTRODUCTION

Recall that literary devices are defined as "rules of thumb, convention, or structure that are employed in literature and storytelling." Like the great Merlin casting a spell, the next four lessons conjure up instances of allusion in poetry.

1. Rhyming
2. Alliteration
3. Simile
4. Metaphor
5. Personification
6. Foreshadowing
7. **Allusion**
8. Hyperbole
9. Onomatopoeia

Allusion is a literary device whereby an author makes a reference to something supposed to be known by the reader, but not explicitly mentioned. For example:

Allusion Example	Reference
He imagined the beautiful, extensive garden was something like Adam and Eve once inhabited.	The Garden of Eden in the Bible
The girls set off on a raft down the small stream, like Tom and Huck on the great Mississippi.	"The Adventures of Tom Sawyer," by Mark Twain
With their tragic deaths, Emma and Max became star-crossed lovers.	William Shakespeare's play, "Romeo and Juliet."
Climbing the hill was a Herculean task for Billy, who struggled with a limp.	The Roman god Hercules, who had great strength and courage and completed 12 great feats.
The furious woman's hair writhed in the wind like snakes. When the scared boy looked upon her, he froze, as if turned into stone.	Medusa, a monster from Greek mythology who had snakes for hair and turned those who looked upon her into stone.
My grandfather clung so tightly to his money, I often expected him to break into a bitter, "Bah Humbug!"	Miserly Scrooge from Charles Dickens' "A Christmas Carol" says, "Bah Humbug" in the novel.

LESSON 25: "FIRE AND ICE" BY ROBERT FROST (ALLUSION)

FEATURED POEM

Some say the world will end in fire,

Some say in ice.

From what I've tasted of desire

I hold with those who favor fire.

But if it had to perish twice,

I think I know enough of hate

To know that for destruction ice

Is also great

And would suffice.

SYNOPSIS

In "Fire and Ice," Robert Frost ponders whether fire or ice will bring about the end of the world. He remarks that either will do, but he believes fire will win out. Frost makes what some see as an allusion to the Bible in the poem. "Some say the world will end in fire," may be linked to Peter 3:7, which states, "the present heavens and earth are reserved for fire, being kept for the day of judgment." In the Bible, the day of judgement is the final trial of all humankind, when each is rewarded or punished according to his or her merits. Frost makes a second scientific allusion that the world may end in ice, perhaps due to our ever-expanding universe. An alternative interpretation of the poem advocates that fire stands for desire and ice for hatred. Either too much desire or too much hatred could potentially bring about the end of humanity via means such as nuclear warfare.

RECITE POEM, TITLE, AND POET

Practice reciting the poem, the poem title, and the name of the poet.

NARRATE THE POEM

COMPLETE COPYWORK

Some say the world will end in fire,
Some say in ice.
From what I've tasted of desire
I hold with those who favor fire.

ELEMENTARY POETRY VOLUME 5: LITERARY DEVICES

COMPLETE DICTATION

_____

_____

_____

_____

DEVICE IDENTIFICATION AND EMPLOYMENT

1. Recite the examples and identify the allusions.
    a. The little boy lined up his toy animals in pairs, like the animals going onto the Ark.
    _____

    b. He loved her as much as Lancelot loved Guinevere.
    _____

    c. Cupid must have hit her with his bow. She's head over heels for him.
    _____

    d. Her lips curved into a Mona Lisa smile.
    _____

2. Find a few examples of alliteration in the poem

3. Identify the Poetic Devices
    a. Circle the instances of allusion in the poem.
    b. Assign letters to the sentences to reveal the rhyming scheme.

	Rhyming Scheme (e.g. A-A-B-B)
Some say the world will end in fire,	( )
Some say in ice.	( )
From what I've tasted of desire	( )
I hold with those who favor fire.	( )
But if it had to perish twice,	( )
I think I know enough of hate	( )
To know that for destruction ice	( )
Is also great	( )
And would suffice.	( )

4. Complete the following sentences containing allusions to works of literature.

   a. Sarah felt like Alice in Wonderland when she _____
   _____.

   b. I imagined his Pinocchio nose growing when he _____
   _____.

   c. The girl _____, just
   like Dorothy in the Wizard of Oz.

   d. Like the Star of Bethlehem, _____
   _____.

CREATE NOVEL ARTWORK (Draw a scene including both fire and ice.)

LESSON 26: "THE WORLD IS TOO MUCH WITH US" BY WILLIAM WORDSWORTH (ALLUSION)

FEATURED POEM

The world is too much with us; late and soon,
Getting and spending, we lay waste our powers;
Little we see in Nature that is ours;
We have given our hearts away, a sordid boon!
This Sea that bares her bosom to the moon;
The winds that will be howling at all hours,
And are up-gathered now like sleeping flowers;
For this, for everything, we are out of tune;

It moves us not. Great God! I'd rather be
A Pagan suckled in a creed outworn;
So might I, standing on this pleasant lea,
Have glimpses that would make me less forlorn;
Have sight of Proteus rising from the sea;
Or hear old Triton blow his wreathèd horn.

Greek God of the Sea Proteus

SYNOPSIS

William Wordsworth wrote "The World Is Too Much with Us" around 1802, in the midst of the First Industrial Revolution (circa 1760-1840). The first eight lines of the poem discuss problems caused by the Industrial Revolution, and the final six lines address the solution. Wordsworth criticizes humankind's elevation of consumerism and rejection of nature. He remarks he'd rather live in a Pagan, nature-worshipping world than a world full of greed and the destruction of nature. Wordsworth alludes to figures in Greek mythology, including Proteus, god of the sea, and Triton, messenger of the sea.

RECITE POEM, TITLE, AND POET

Practice reciting the poem, the poem title, and the name of the poet.

NARRATE THE POEM

COMPLETE COPYWORK

The world is too much with us; late and soon,
Getting and spending, we lay waste our powers;
Little we see in Nature that is ours;

COMPLETE DICTATION

_____

_____

_____

DEVICE IDENTIFICATION AND EMPLOYMENT

1. Recite the examples and identify the allusions.

    a. The arboretum was a Garden of Eden.

    _____

    b. Be careful up there. You don't want to fly too close to the sun.

    _____

    c. His teeth gleamed, his enormous smile overtaking his face like the Cheshire Cat's.

    _____

    d. Adorable puppies are my Kryptonite.

    _____

2. Find a few examples of alliteration from the poem.

3. Locate an example of a simile in the poem, naming the compared pairs of elements.

4. Discover any personified objects.

5. Identify the Poetic Devices

    a. Circle the instances of allusion in the poem excerpt.
    b. Assign letters to the sentences to reveal the rhyming scheme.

	Rhyming Scheme (e.g. A-A-B-B)
It moves us not. Great God! I'd rather be	( )
A Pagan suckled in a creed outworn;	( )
So might I, standing on this pleasant lea,	( )
Have glimpses that would make me less forlorn;	( )
Have sight of Proteus rising from the sea;	( )
Or hear old Triton blow his wreathèd horn.	( )

6. Complete the following sentences containing allusions to works of literature.

   a. When I _____
      the little boy stared at me and said, "You must be good witch like Glinda!"

   b. The boy looked worried because _____
      so I tossed him my phone and said, "Why don't you phone home, like the alien?"

   c. Just like Cinderella, she _____
      _____.

   d. I called the little girl Tarzan because _____
      _____.

CREATE NOVEL ARTWORK (Contrast the natural world with industrialization in a drawing.)

ELEMENTARY POETRY VOLUME 5: LITERARY DEVICES

LESSON 27: "CHRISTMAS DAY" BY CHRISTINA ROSSETTI (ALLUSION)

FEATURED POEM

A baby is a harmless thing
    And wins our hearts with one accord,
And Flower of Babies was their King,
    Jesus Christ our Lord:
Lily of lilies He
Upon His Mother's knee;
Rose of roses, soon to be
Crowned with thorns on leafless tree.

A lamb is innocent and mild
    And merry on the soft green sod;
And Jesus Christ, the Undefiled,
    Is the Lamb of God:
Only spotless He
Upon His Mother's knee;
White and ruddy, soon to be
Sacrificed for you and me.

Nay, lamb is not so sweet a word,
    Nor lily half so pure a name;
Another name our hearts hath stirred,
    Kindling them to flame:
"Jesus" certainly
Is music and melody:
Heart with heart in harmony
Carol we and worship we.

SYNOPSIS

Christina Rossetti's "Christmas Day" alludes to the Biblical birth, life, crucifixion, and death of Jesus Christ. Rossetti employs multiple metaphors, comparing Jesus Christ to a lamb, a rose, and a lily. Rossetti also uses rhyming for effect.

RECITE POEM, TITLE, AND POET

Practice reciting the poem, the poem title, and the name of the poet.

NARRATE THE POEM

_____

_____

_____

_____

COMPLETE COPYWORK

Only spotless He
Upon His Mother's knee;
White and ruddy, soon to be
Sacrificed for you and me.

_____

_____

_____

_____

COMPLETE DICTATION

_____

_____

_____

_____

DEVICE IDENTIFICATION AND EMPLOYMENT

1. Recite the examples and identify the allusions.

   a. She's got the Midas touch. Every business she starts makes money.
   _____

   b. Hey, where did she go? People come and go so quickly here.
   _____

   c. Forgive your brother. Turn the other cheek.
   _____

   d. Chocolate donuts were his Achilles' Heel.
   _____

2. Find a few examples of alliteration from the poem.

3. Locate an example of a metaphor in the poem, naming the compared pairs of elements.

4. Identify the Poetic Devices
   a. Circle the instances of allusion in the poem excerpt.
   b. Assign letters to the sentences to reveal the rhyming scheme.

	Rhyming Scheme (e.g. A-A-B-B)
And wins our hearts with one accord,	( )
And Flower of Babies was their King,	( )
Jesus Christ our Lord:	( )
Lily of lilies He	( )
Upon His Mother's knee;	( )
Rose of roses, soon to be	( )
Crowned with thorns on leafless tree.	( )

5. Write a poem of six lines, incorporating at least one allusion and the couplet rhyming scheme.

_____ (A)

_____ (A)

_____ (B)

_____ (B)

_____ (C)

_____ (C)

CREATE NOVEL ARTWORK (Illustrate your family's Christmas or other holiday celebration.)

LESSON 28: "THE LADY OF SHALOTT"
BY ALFRED LORD TENNYSON (ALLUSION)

FEATURED POEM

Part I

1. On either side the river lie
Long fields of barley and of rye,
That clothe the wold and meet the sky;
And thro' the field the road runs by
   To many-tower'd Camelot;
And up and down the people go,
Gazing where the lilies blow
Round an island there below,
   The island of Shalott.

2. Willows whiten, aspens quiver.
Little breezes dusk and shiver
Thro' the wave that runs for ever
By the island in the river
   Flowing down to Camelot.
Four gray walls, and four gray towers
Overlook a space of flowers,
And the silent isle imbowers
   The Lady of Shalott.

3. By the margin, willow veil'd,
Slide the heavy barges trail'd
By slow horses; and unhail'd
The shallop flitteth silken-sail'd
   Skimming down to Camelot:
But who hath seen her wave her hand?
Or at the casement seen her stand?
Or is she known in all the land,
   The Lady of Shalott?

4. Only reapers, reaping early
In among the bearded barley,
Hear a song that echoes cheerly
From the river winding clearly,
   Down to tower'd Camelot:
And by the moon the reaper weary,
Piling sheaves in uplands airy,
Listening, whispers "'Tis the fairy
   Lady of Shalott."

Part II

5. There she weaves by night and day
A magic web with colours gay.
She has heard a whisper say,
A curse is on her if she stay
   To look down to Camelot.
She knows not what the curse may be,
And so she weaveth steadily,
And little other care hath she,
   The Lady of Shalott.

6. And moving thro' a mirror clear
That hangs before her all the year,
Shadows of the world appear.
There she sees the highway near
   Winding down to Camelot:
There the river eddy whirls,
And there the surly village-churls,
And the red cloaks of market girls,
   Pass onward from Shalott.

7. Sometimes a troop of damsels glad,
An abbot on an ambling pad,
Sometimes a curly shepherd-lad,
Or long-hair'd page in crimson clad,
   Goes by to tower'd Camelot;
And sometimes thro' the mirror blue
The knights come riding two and two:
She hath no loyal knight and true,
   The Lady of Shalott.

8. But in her web she still delights
To weave the mirror's magic sights,
For often thro' the silent nights
A funeral, with plumes and lights
   And music, went to Camelot:
Or when the moon was overhead,
Came two young lovers lately wed:
"I am half sick of shadows," said
   The Lady of Shalott.

Part III
9. A bow-shot from her bower-eaves,
He rode between the barley-sheaves,
The sun came dazzling thro' the leaves,
And flamed upon the brazen greaves
   Of bold Sir Lancelot.
A red-cross knight for ever kneel'd
To a lady in his shield,
That sparkled on the yellow field,
   Beside remote Shalott.

10. The gemmy bridle glitter'd free,
Like to some branch of stars we see
Hung in the golden Galaxy.
The bridle bells rang merrily
   As he rode down to Camelot:
And from his blazon'd baldric slung
A mighty silver bugle hung,
And as he rode his armour rung,
   Beside remote Shalott.

11. All in the blue unclouded weather
Thick-jewell'd shone the saddle-leather,
The helmet and the helmet-feather
Burn'd like one burning flame together,
   As he rode down to Camelot.
As often thro' the purple night,
Below the starry clusters bright,
Some bearded meteor, trailing light,
   Moves over still Shalott.

12. His broad clear brow in sunlight glow'd;
On burnish'd hooves his war-horse trode;
From underneath his helmet flow'd
His coal-black curls as on he rode,
   As he rode down to Camelot.
From the bank and from the river
He flash'd into the crystal mirror,
"Tirra lirra," by the river
   Sang Sir Lancelot.

13. She left the web, she left the loom,
She made three paces thro' the room,
She saw the water-lily bloom,
She saw the helmet and the plume,
   She look'd down to Camelot.
Out flew the web and floated wide;
The mirror crack'd from side to side;
"The curse is come upon me," cried
   The Lady of Shalott.

Part IV

14. In the stormy east-wind straining,
The pale yellow woods were waning,
The broad stream in his banks complaining,
Heavily the low sky raining
   Over tower'd Camelot;
Down she came and found a boat
Beneath a willow left afloat,
And round about the prow she wrote
   The Lady of Shalott.

15. And down the river's dim expanse
Like some bold seër in a trance,
Seeing all his own mischance—
With a glassy countenance
   Did she look to Camelot.
And at the closing of the day
She loosed the chain, and down she lay;
The broad stream bore her far away,
   The Lady of Shalott.

16. Lying, robed in snowy white
That loosely flew to left and right—
The leaves upon her falling light—
Thro' the noises of the night
   She floated down to Camelot:
And as the boat-head wound along
The willowy hills and fields among,
They heard her singing her last song,
   The Lady of Shalott.

17. Heard a carol, mournful, holy,
Chanted loudly, chanted lowly,
Till her blood was frozen slowly,
And her eyes were darken'd wholly,
   Turn'd to tower'd Camelot.
For ere she reach'd upon the tide
The first house by the water-side,
Singing in her song she died,
   The Lady of Shalott.

18. Under tower and balcony,
By garden-wall and gallery,
A gleaming shape she floated by,
Dead-pale between the houses high,
   Silent into Camelot.
Out upon the wharfs they came,
Knight and burgher, lord and dame,
And round the prow they read her name,
   The Lady of Shalott.

19. Who is this? and what is here?
And in the lighted palace near
Died the sound of royal cheer;
And they cross'd themselves for fear,
   All the knights at Camelot:
But Lancelot mused a little space;
He said, "She has a lovely face;
God in his mercy lend her grace,
   The Lady of Shalott."

SYNOPSIS

Alfred Lord Tennyson's poem, "The Lady of Shalott," alludes to the medieval mythological tales of King Arthur and his castle and court of Camelot. In Arthurian legend, a woman named Elaine is smitten with Sir Lancelot, one of King Arthur's Knights of the Round Table. When Elaine confesses her love, Sir Lancelot rejects her. Dying from a broken heart, Elaine instructs her father to float her body on a river barge to Camelot. When her body arrives, Sir Lancelot is grieved. However, he does not regret refusing Elaine's advances because he does not love her. Although featuring a similar storyline, the poem differs from the traditional tale. In the poem version, "The Lady of Shalott" is imprisoned on the Isle of Shalott, which sits in the midst of a river flowing to Camelot. The Lady of Shalott is forced to spin a magic web and will be cursed if she looks at Camelot. She can only view shadowy reflections of Camelot and its people through a magical mirror. One day, the Lady of Shalott spots Sir Lancelot floating by on the river. She falls so deeply in love with him that she looks at Camelot and is cursed. Knowing she is cursed, she lies in a barge and floats down the river to Camelot. By the time she reaches Camelot, she's perished from the cold. Sir Lancelot sees her and remarks, "She has a lovely face; God in his mercy lend her grace, The Lady of Shalott."

RECITE POEM, TITLE, AND POET

Practice reciting the poem, the poem title, and the name of the poet.

NARRATE THE POEM

_____

_____

_____

_____

COMPLETE COPYWORK

God in his mercy lend her grace,
The Lady of Shalott.

_____

_____

COMPLETE DICTATION

_____

_____

DEVICE IDENTIFICATION AND EMPLOYMENT

1. Recite the examples and identify the allusions.

   a. I can't find her anywhere. I guess she put on Arthur's Mantle of Invisibility.
   _____

   b. The heavens swirled more brightly than in "The Starry Night."
   _____

   c. You might want to rethink your actions. You don't want to open Pandora's box.
   _____

   d. Shocking the other kids, the small boy defeated the bully, like David triumphing over Goliath.
   _____

2. Find a few examples of similes in the poem, naming the compared pairs of elements.

3. Locate an example of foreshadowing in the poem.

4. Identify the Poetic Devices
   a. Circle the instances of allusion in the poem excerpt.
   b. Assign letters to the sentences to reveal the rhyming scheme.

   Rhyming Scheme (e.g. A-A-B-B)

Line	Scheme
Who is this? and what is here?	( )
And in the lighted palace near	( )
Died the sound of royal cheer;	( )
And they cross'd themselves for fear,	( )
All the knights at Camelot:	( )
But Lancelot mused a little space;	( )
He said, "She has a lovely face;	( )
God in his mercy lend her grace,	( )
The Lady of Shalott."	( )

5. Write a poem of six lines, incorporating at least one allusion and the triplet rhyming scheme.

_____ (A)

_____ (A)

_____ (A)

_____ (B)

_____ (B)

_____ (B)

CREATE NOVEL ARTWORK (Draw "The Lady of Shalott" approaching Camelot.)

ELEMENTARY POETRY VOLUME 5: LITERARY DEVICES

PART VIII: HYPERBOLE

INTRODUCTION

Recall that literary devices are defined as "rules of thumb, convention, or structure that are employed in literature and storytelling." The next four lessons embark into the greatest in-depth investigation of hyperbole in the history of poetry!

1. Rhyming
2. Alliteration
3. Simile
4. Metaphor
5. Personification
6. Foreshadowing
7. Allusion
8. **Hyperbole**
9. Onomatopoeia

Hyperbole is a literary device whereby an author makes a deliberate or unintentional overstatement. For example:

Hyperbole Example	Explanation
The baby screams were the loudest sounds in the universe.	The screams might be loud, but certainly not the loudest sounds in the universe.
I'll just die if I don't get a cup of coffee this morning.	You may be grumpy and suffering from caffeine withdrawal without coffee, but you will likely not die.
I'm going to burst if I eat one more bite.	If you eat one more bite, you may feel awful, but you likely will not break your stomach.
You are the best dog is the whole world.	We all love our dogs, but they are likely not the "best in the world" by objective metrics. However, they can certainly subjectively be the best to us.
He's sucking all of the life right out of me.	He may be stressing you out, but not literally taking all of your life.
You scared me to death!	As you are still alive to produce this sentiment, you were not literally scared to death.
He was a giant among men.	He might be great and awe-inspiring, but he isn't literally a twenty-foot tall giant.

LESSON 29: "CONCORD HYMN" BY RALPH WALDO EMERSON (HYPERBOLE)

FEATURED POEM

By the rude bridge that arched the flood,
    Their flag to April's breeze unfurled,
Here once the embattled farmers stood
    And fired the shot heard round the world.

The foe long since in silence slept;
    Alike the conqueror silent sleeps;
And Time the ruined bridge has swept
    Down the dark stream which seaward creeps.

On this green bank, by this soft stream,
    We set today a votive stone;
That memory may their deed redeem,
    When, like our sires, our sons are gone.

Spirit, that made those heroes dare
    To die, and leave their children free,
Bid Time and Nature gently spare
    The shaft we raise to them and thee.

SYNOPSIS

Ralph Waldo Emerson's poem, "Concord Hymn," alludes to the first shot fired in the Revolutionary War by an American militiaman at the British troops in Concord, Massachusetts. The first shot occurred in April, as referred to in the poem. Emerson employs hyperbole when he calls the first shot, "the shot heard round the world." Obviously, not everyone in the world heard it. However, the Revolutionary War has had a world-wide impact, changing the trajectory of world events since that time.

RECITE POEM, TITLE, AND POET

Practice reciting the poem, the poem title, and the name of the poet.

NARRATE THE POEM

_____

_____

_____

_____

_____

_____

COMPLETE COPYWORK

By the rude bridge that arched the flood,
Their flag to April's breeze unfurled,
Here once the embattled farmers stood
And fired the shot heard round the world.

_____

_____

_____

_____

COMPLETE DICTATION

_____

_____

_____

_____

_____

DEVICE IDENTIFICATION AND EMPLOYMENT

1. Recite the sentences and explain why they exemplify hyperbole.

    a. You're taking forever!
    _____

    b. Back in my day, I had to walk fifty miles to school and it was uphill both ways.
    _____

    c. I can't believe you won't let me take the car, Mom. I'm never going to speak to you again!
    _____

    d. Stop it with the cheesy jokes. You're killing me!
    _____

2. Find a few examples of alliteration in the poem.

3. Identify the Poetic Devices
    a. Circle the instances of hyperbole in the poem excerpt.
    b. Assign letters to the sentences to reveal the rhyming scheme.

	Rhyming Scheme (e.g. A-A-B-B)
By the rude bridge that arched the flood,	( )
Their flag to April's breeze unfurled,	( )
Here once the embattled farmers stood	( )
And fired the shot heard round the world.	( )
The foe long since in silence slept;	( )
Alike the conqueror silent sleeps;	( )
And Time the ruined bridge has swept	( )
Down the dark stream which seaward creeps.	( )

4. Complete the following sentences to incorporate hyperbole.

   a. She turned cartwheels as fast as _____.

   b. He grew as tall as a _____.

   c. I'm so hungry, I could eat a _____.

   d. She ran so fast _____.

   e. I'm so tired, I could _____.

CREATE NOVEL ARTWORK (Write a hyperbolic statement and illustrate its exaggeration.)

Hyperbolic Statement:
Illustration:

LESSON 30: "A RED, RED ROSE" BY ROBERT BURNS (HYPERBOLE)

FEATURED POEM

O my Love is like a red, red rose

That's newly sprung in June;

O my Love is like the melody

That's sweetly played in tune.

As fair art thou, my bonnie lass,

So deep in love am I;

And I will love thee still, my dear,

Till a' the seas gang dry.

Till a' the seas gang dry, my dear,

And the rocks melt wi' the sun;

I will love thee still, my dear,

While the sands o' life shall run.

And fare thee weel, my only love!

And fare thee weel awhile!

And I will come again, my love,

Though it were ten thousand mile.

SYNOPSIS

"A Red, Red Rose" by Robert Burns incorporates hyperbole to express the narrator's love for his "bonnie lass." He will love her until the seas go dry and the rocks melt in the sun. The end of the poem reveals the narrator must part from his love, but assures the reader that he'd travel ten thousand miles for their reunion.

RECITE POEM, TITLE, AND POET

Practice reciting the poem, the poem title, and the name of the poet.

NARRATE THE POEM

_____

_____

_____

_____

_____

COMPLETE COPYWORK

O my Love is like a red, red rose
That's newly sprung in June;
O my Love is like the melody
That's sweetly played in tune.

_____

_____

_____

COMPLETE DICTATION

_____

_____

_____

_____

_____

DEVICE IDENTIFICATION AND EMPLOYMENT

1. Recite the sentences and explain why they exemplify hyperbole.

    a. I ate a million pancakes.

    _____

    b. I'm so hungry I could eat a whole cow.

    _____

    c. I love you so much, I'd travel to Jupiter for you.

    _____

2. Find two examples of similes in the poem.

3. Identify the Poetic Devices

    a. Circle the instances of hyperbole in the poem excerpt.
    b. Assign letters to the sentences to reveal the rhyming scheme.

	Rhyming Scheme (e.g. A-A-B-B)
As fair art thou, my bonnie lass,	( )
So deep in love am I;	( )
And I will love thee still, my dear,	( )
Till a' the seas gang dry.	( )
Till a' the seas gang dry, my dear,	( )
And the rocks melt wi' the sun;	( )
I will love thee still, my dear,	( )
While the sands o' life shall run.	( )

4. Complete the following sentences to incorporate hyperbole.

    a. I ate as much as _____.

    b. He walked so slow _____.

    c. The ice skater spun faster _____.

    d. The bag was a heavy as a _____.

    e. It snowed so much _____.

CREATE NOVEL ARTWORK (Draw an exaggeration of your love for an object or a person.)

LESSON 31: "CASEY AT THE BAT"
BY ERNEST LAWRENCE THAYER (HYPERBOLE)

FEATURED POEM

1. It looked extremely rocky for the Mudville nine that day:
The score stood four to six with just an inning left to play;
And so, when Cooney died at first, and Burrows did the same,
A pallor wreathed the features of the patrons of the game.

2. A straggling few got up to go, leaving there the rest
With that hope that springs eternal within the human breast;
For they thought if only Casey could get one whack, at that
They'd put up even money, with Casey at the bat.

3. But Flynn preceded Casey, and so likewise did Blake,
But the former was a pudding, and the latter was a fake;
And so, on that stricken multitude a death-like silence sat,
For there seemed but little chance of Casey's getting to the bat.

4. But Flynn let drive a single to the wonderment of all,
And the much-despisèd Blaikie tore the cover off the ball;
And when the dust had settled, and they saw what had occurred,
There was Blaikie safe on second and Flynn a-hugging third!

5. Then from the gladdened multitude went up a joyous yell,
It bounded from the mountain-top, and rattled in the dell,
It struck upon the hillside, and rebounded on the flat;
For Casey, mighty Casey, was advancing to the bat.

6. There was ease in Casey's manner as he stepped into his place,
There was pride in Casey's bearing, and a smile on Casey's face;
And when, responding to the cheers, he lightly doffed his hat,
No stranger in the crowd could doubt 'twas Casey at the bat.

7. Ten thousand eyes were on him as he rubbed his hands with dirt,
Five thousand tongues applauded when he wiped them on his shirt;
Then, while the writhing pitcher ground the ball into his hip,
Defiance glanced in Casey's eye, a sneer curled Casey's lip.

8. And now the leather-covered sphere came hurtling through the air,
And Casey stood a-watching it in haughty grandeur there;
Close by the sturdy batsman the ball unheeded sped:
"That ain't my style," said Casey. "Strike one," the umpire said.

9. From the benches, black with people, there went up a muffled roar,
Like the beating of the storm-waves on a stern and distant shore;
"Kill him! Kill the umpire!" shouted someone in the stand.
And it's likely they'd have killed him had not Casey raised his hand.

10. With a smile of Christian charity great Casey's visage shone;
He stilled the rising tumult; he bade the game go on;
He signaled to the pitcher, and once more the spheroid flew,
But Casey still ignored it; and the umpire said, "Strike two."

11. "Fraud!" cried the maddened thousands, and the echo answered, "Fraud!"
But the scornful look from Casey, and the audience was awed;
They saw his face grow stern and cold, they saw his muscles strain,
And they knew that Casey wouldn't let that ball go by again.

12. The sneer is gone from Casey's lip, his teeth are clenched with hate;
He pounds with cruel violence his bat upon the plate;
And now the pitcher holds the ball, and now he lets it go,
And now the air is shattered by the force of Casey's blow.

13. Oh, somewhere in this favored land the sun is shining bright,
The band is playing somewhere, and somewhere hearts are light,
And somewhere men are laughing, and somewhere children shout;
But there is no joy in Mudville—mighty Casey has struck out.

SYNOPSIS

The featured poem describes the desperate situation of the Mudville baseball team. It's the final inning, and Mudville must score or lose the game. Mudville is currently down, six to four. Two batters have struck out, one is on second base, and another is on third base. Luckily for the Mudville team, Casey, the team's superstar, is up to bat. Casey lets the first two pitches go by without swinging, racking up two strikes. One more strike, and Mudville will lose the game. Will Casey knock it out of the park? Will Casey strike out? The poem reveals the answer. The poem leverages hyperbole for effect, for example, stating if Casey had not raised his hand, the crowd would have likely have killed the umpire.

RECITE POEM, TITLE, AND POET

Practice reciting the poem, the poem title, and the name of the poet.

NARRATE THE POEM

___

___

___

___

___

___

COMPLETE COPYWORK

And somewhere men are laughing, and somewhere children shout;
But there is no joy in Mudville—mighty Casey has struck out.

___

___

___

COMPLETE DICTATION

_____

_____

_____

DEVICE IDENTIFICATION AND EMPLOYMENT

1. Recite the sentences and explain why they exemplify hyperbole.

    a. My love for your burns brighter than a million suns.
    _____

    b. My backpack weighs a ton.
    _____

    c. He's as tall as a mountain.
    _____

    d. She's as timid as a mouse.
    _____

2. Locate a few occurrences of alliteration in the poem.

3. Find two examples of similes from the poem.

4. Identify the Poetic Devices
    a. Circle the instances of hyperbole in the poem excerpt.
    b. Assign letters to the sentences to reveal the rhyming scheme.

	<u>Rhyming Scheme (e.g. A-A-B-B)</u>
From the benches, black with people, there went up a muffled roar,	( )
Like the beating of the storm-waves on a stern and distant shore;	( )
"Kill him! Kill the umpire!" shouted someone in the stand.	( )
And it's likely they'd have killed him had not Casey raised his hand.	( )
The sneer is gone from Casey's lip, his teeth are clenched with hate;	( )
He pounds with cruel violence his bat upon the plate;	( )
And now the pitcher holds the ball, and now he lets it go,	( )
And now the air is shattered by the force of Casey's blow.	( )

5. Write a poem of six lines, including at least one instance of hyperbole and the couplet rhyming scheme.

_____ (A)

_____ (A)

_____ (B)

_____ (B)

_____ (C)

_____ (C)

CREATE NOVEL ARTWORK (Sketch an exaggerated representation of one of your accomplishments.)

LESSON 32: "FOR EACH ECSTATIC INSTANT" BY EMILY DICKINSON (HYPERBOLE)

FEATURED POEM

For each ecstatic instant
We must an anguish pay
In keen and quivering ratio
To the ecstasy.

For each beloved hour
Sharp pittances of years —
Bitter contested farthings —
And Coffers heaped with Tears!

SYNOPSIS

Emily Dickinson's "For Each Ecstatic Instant" uses hyperbole to express the grief of the narrator, describing "coffers heaped with tears." Imagine how much you would have to cry to fill up a box. The poem expresses that in life, we must pay in pain to purchase our joys.

RECITE POEM, TITLE, AND POET

Practice reciting the poem, the poem title, and the name of the poet.

NARRATE THE POEM

COMPLETE COPYWORK

For each ecstatic instant
We must an anguish pay
In keen and quivering ratio
To the ecstasy.

COMPLETE DICTATION

_____

_____

_____

_____

DEVICE IDENTIFICATION AND EMPLOYMENT

1. Recite the sentences and explain why they exemplify hyperbole.

   a. It's so chilly in our house, Polar Bears will want to move in.

   _____

   b. So many mosquitos bit me, I don't have a drop of blood left.

   _____

   c. I'm so tired I could sleep for a thousand years.

   _____

2. Find an instance of alliteration from the poem.

3. Identify the Poetic Devices

   a. Circle the instances of hyperbole in the poem excerpt.
   b. Assign letters to the sentences to reveal the rhyming scheme.

Rhyming Scheme (e.g. A-A-B-B)

For each ecstatic instant	( )
We must an anguish pay	( )
In keen and quivering ratio	( )
To the ecstasy.	( )
For each beloved hour	( )
Sharp pittances of years —	( )
Bitter contested farthings —	( )
And coffers heaped with tears!	( )

4. Write a poem of six lines, incorporating at least one instance of hyperbole and the traditional rhyming scheme.

_____ (A)

_____ (B)

_____ (A)

_____ (B)

_____ (A)

_____ (B)

CREATE NOVEL ARTWORK (Illustrate "coffers heaped with tears.")

ELEMENTARY POETRY VOLUME 5: LITERARY DEVICES

PART IX: ONOMATOPOEIA

INTRODUCTION

Recall that literary devices are defined as "rules of thumb, convention, or structure that are employed in literature and storytelling." The final four lessons present the tinkle, the tap, the rustle, and the buzz of onomatopoeia.

1. Rhyming
2. Alliteration
3. Simile
4. Metaphor
5. Personification
6. Foreshadowing
7. Allusion
8. Hyperbole
9. **Onomatopoeia**

Onomatopoeia is a literary device whereby an author uses a word that sounds like what it represents, such as "gurgle" or "moo." Recite the examples listed in the table to get a sense for onomatopoeic words.

Onomatopoeic Words		
Achoo	Slam	Purr
Crunch	Splash	Blurt
Bam	Mumble	Whisper
Pop	Burble	Thump
Whir	Glug	Bang
Belch	Whack	Chickadee
Burp	Clunk	Cuckoo
Crash	Crack	Murmur
Honk	Beep	Fizz
Clang	Vroom	Splat
Boing	Zip	Boom
Shush	Giggle	Zap
Growl	Whine	Tick-tock

LESSON 33: "THE BELLS"
BY EDGAR ALLAN POE (ONOMATOPOEIA)

FEATURED POEM

VERSE I

Hear the sledges with the bells—

Silver bells!

What a world of merriment their melody foretells!

How they tinkle, tinkle, tinkle,

In the icy air of night!

While the stars that oversprinkle

All the heavens, seem to twinkle

With a crystalline delight;

Keeping time, time, time,

In a sort of Runic rhyme,

To the tintinabulation that so musically wells

From the bells, bells, bells, bells,

Bells, bells, bells—

From the jingling and the tinkling of the bells.

VERSE II

Hear the mellow wedding bells,

Golden bells!

What a world of happiness their harmony foretells!

Through the balmy air of night

How they ring out their delight!

From the molten-golden notes,

And all in tune,

What a liquid ditty floats

To the turtle-dove that listens, while she gloats

On the moon!

Oh, from out the sounding cells,

What a gush of euphony voluminously wells!

How it swells!

How it dwells

On the Future! how it tells

Of the rapture that impels

To the swinging and the ringing

Of the bells, bells, bells,

Of the bells, bells, bells, bells,

Bells, bells, bells—

To the rhyming and the chiming of the bells!

VERSE III

Hear the loud alarum bells—
Brazen bells!
What tale of terror, now, their turbulency tells!
In the startled ear of night
How they scream out their affright!
Too much horrified to speak,
They can only shriek, shriek,
Out of tune,
In a clamorous appealing to the mercy of the fire,
In a mad expostulation with the deaf and frantic fire,
Leaping higher, higher, higher,
With a desperate desire,
And a resolute endeavor
Now—now to sit or never,
By the side of the pale-faced moon.
Oh, the bells, bells, bells!
What a tale their terror tells
Of Despair!
How they clang, and clash, and roar!

What a horror they outpour
On the bosom of the palpitating air!
Yet the ear it fully knows,
By the twanging,
And the clanging,
How the danger ebbs and flows;
Yet the ear distinctly tells,
In the jangling,
And the wrangling.
How the danger sinks and swells,
By the sinking or the swelling in the anger of the bells—
Of the bells—
Of the bells, bells, bells, bells,
Bells, bells, bells—
In the clamor and the clangor of the bells!

VERSE IV

Hear the tolling of the bells—

Iron bells!

What a world of solemn thought their monody compels!

In the silence of the night,

How we shiver with affright

At the melancholy menace of their tone!

For every sound that floats

From the rust within their throats

Is a groan.

And the people—ah, the people—

They that dwell up in the steeple,

All alone,

And who tolling, tolling, tolling,

In that muffled monotone,

Feel a glory in so rolling

On the human heart a stone—

They are neither man nor woman—

They are neither brute nor human—

They are Ghouls:

And their king it is who tolls;

And he rolls, rolls, rolls,
Rolls
A pæan from the bells!
And his merry bosom swells
With the pæan of the bells!
And he dances, and he yells;
Keeping time, time, time,
In a sort of Runic rhyme,
To the pæan of the bells—
Of the bells:
Keeping time, time, time,
In a sort of Runic rhyme,
To the throbbing of the bells—
Of the bells, bells, bells—
To the sobbing of the bells;
Keeping time, time, time,
As he knells, knells, knells,
In a happy Runic rhyme,
To the rolling of the bells—
Of the bells, bells, bells—
To the tolling of the bells,
Of the bells, bells, bells, bells—
Bells, bells, bells—
To the moaning and the groaning of the bells.

SYNOPSIS

Edgar Allan Poe sprinkles onomatopoetic terms liberally through his poem, "The Bells." Poe describes in detail the joyous, celebratory, panicked, and sorrowful ringing of different types of bells. Poe first describes the joyful tinkling and jingling of sleigh bells, second, the equally happy but mellow ringing and chiming of wedding bells, third, the clanging and shrieking of alarm bells, and finally, the mournful moaning and groaning of iron bells.

RECITE POEM, TITLE, AND POET

Practice reciting the poem, the poem title, and the name of the poet.

NARRATE THE POEM

_____

_____

_____

_____

_____

_____

_____

COMPLETE COPYWORK

Hear the sledges with the bells—
Silver bells!
What a world of merriment their melody foretells!

_____

_____

_____

_____

ELEMENTARY POETRY VOLUME 5: LITERARY DEVICES

COMPLETE DICTATION

_____

_____

_____

_____

DEVICE IDENTIFICATION AND EMPLOYMENT

1. Circle the onomatopoetic words in the sentences below.

    a. The bag of grain hit the ground with a thud.

    b. The bee buzzed around the red and yellow tulips.

    c. The cat rubbed against my legs and meowed.

    d. The baseball bat smacked the baseball out of the park.

2. Find a few occurrences of alliteration in the poem.

3. Locate a few examples of personification in the poem.

4. Identify the Poetic Devices

    a. Circle the instances of onomatopoeia in the poem excerpt.
    b. Assign letters to the sentences to reveal the rhyming scheme.

	Rhyming Scheme (e.g. A-A-B-B)
The earth is just so full of fun	( )
Hear the sledges with the bells—	( )
Silver bells!	( )
What a world of merriment their melody foretells!	( )
How they tinkle, tinkle, tinkle,	( )
In the icy air of night!	( )
While the stars that oversprinkle	( )
All the heavens, seem to twinkle	( )
With a crystalline delight;	( )
Keeping time, time, time,	( )
In a sort of Runic rhyme,	( )
To the tintinabulation that so musically wells	( )
From the jingling and the tinkling of the bells.	( )

5. Write a poem of six lines, incorporating at least one instance of onomatopoeia and the traditional rhyming scheme.

_____ (A)

_____ (B)

_____ (A)

_____ (B)

_____ (A)

_____ (B)

CREATE NOVEL ARTWORK (Draw a scene incorporating an onomatopoetic word.)

LESSON 34: "MEETING AT NIGHT" BY ROBERT BROWNING (ONOMATOPOEIA)

FEATURED POEM

VERSE I

The grey sea and the long black land;
And the yellow half-moon large and low;
And the startled little waves that leap
In fiery ringlets from their sleep,
As I gain the cove with pushing prow,
And quench its speed i' the slushy sand.

VERSE II

Then a mile of warm sea-scented beach;
Three fields to cross till a farm appears;
A tap at the pane, the quick sharp scratch
And blue spurt of a lighted match,
And a voice less loud, thro' its joys and fears,
Than the two hearts beating each to each!

SYNOPSIS

In "Meeting at Night," Robert Browning immerses the reader in the narrator's journey under a moonlit sky. The narrator rows in a boat, hikes over a sandy beach, and crosses three fields to arrive at a farm for a joyous reunion with a loved one. The poem provides examples of onomatopoeia in describing the narrator's tap at the pane, the scratch of a match, and the spurt of a flame.

RECITE POEM, TITLE, AND POET

Practice reciting the poem, the poem title, and the name of the poet.

NARRATE THE POEM

COMPLETE COPYWORK

Then a mile of warm sea-scented beach;
Three fields to cross till a farm appears;
A tap at the pane, the quick sharp scratch
And blue spurt of a lighted match.

ELEMENTARY POETRY VOLUME 5: LITERARY DEVICES

COMPLETE DICTATION

_____

_____

_____

_____

_____

DEVICE IDENTIFICATION AND EMPLOYMENT

1. Circle the onomatopoetic words in the sentences below.

    a. The old tugboat chugged up the river.

    b. The bottle rocket whizzed up into the sky and exploded with a pop.

    c. He cracked the walnut open.

    d. The kebabs sizzled on the grill.

2. Identify the Poetic Devices
    a. Circle the instances of onomatopoeia in the poem.
    b. Assign letters to the sentences to reveal the rhyming scheme.

	Rhyming Scheme (e.g. A-A-B-B)
The grey sea and the long black land;	( )
And the yellow half-moon large and low;	( )
And the startled little waves that leap	( )
In fiery ringlets from their sleep,	( )
As I gain the cove with pushing prow,	( )
And quench its speed i' the slushy sand.	( )
Then a mile of warm sea-scented beach;	( )
Three fields to cross till a farm appears;	( )
A tap at the pane, the quick sharp scratch	( )
And blue spurt of a lighted match,	( )
And a voice less loud, thro' its joys and fears,	( )
Than the two hearts beating each to each!	( )

3. Write a poem of six lines, incorporating at least one instance of onomatopoeia and the couplet rhyming scheme.

_____ (A)

_____ (A)

_____ (B)

_____ (B)

_____ (C)

_____ (C)

CREATE NOVEL ARTWORK (Draw something you could easily describe with onomatopoeic words.)

LESSON 35: "GATHERING LEAVES" BY ROBERT FROST (ONOMATOPOEIA)

FEATURED POEM

1. Spades take up leaves
No better than spoons,
And bags full of leaves
Are light as balloons.

2. I make a great noise
Of rustling all day
Like rabbit and deer
Running away.

3. But the mountains I raise
Elude my embrace,
Flowing over my arms
And into my face.

4. I may load and unload
Again and again
Till I fill the whole shed,
And what have I then?

5. Next to nothing for weight,
And since they grew duller
From contact with earth,
Next to nothing for color.

6. Next to nothing for use,
But a crop is a crop,
And who's to say where
The harvest shall stop?

SYNOPSIS

In the poem, the narrator describes the tedious process of raking up, bagging, and hauling off mountains of leaves. The narrator complains that spades are no better than tiny spoons for scooping up leaves, and gripes that when he scoops up the leaves with his arms, many overflow to escape back the ground. He forces the mountains of leaves into bags, which when full are as light and inconsequential as balloons, belying the hard work taken to fill them. Even more dispiriting, the leaves he's painstakingly bagged are worthless. The narrator reminds himself that removing the leaves is an essential part of fall harvest time that will allow other plants to flourish in the following spring and summer. The tired narrator wonders whether the continual cycle of trees growing and losing their leaves will ever stop. The poem uses the onomatopoeic word "rustling" to describe the sound of the moving leaves.

RECITE POEM, TITLE, AND POET

Practice reciting the poem, the poem title, and the name of the poet.

NARRATE THE POEM

_____

_____

_____

COMPLETE COPYWORK

But the mountains I raise
Elude my embrace,
Flowing over my arms
And into my face.

_____

_____

_____

ELEMENTARY POETRY VOLUME 5: LITERARY DEVICES

COMPLETE DICTATION

_____

_____

_____

_____

DEVICE IDENTIFICATION AND EMPLOYMENT

1. Circle the onomatopoetic words in the sentences below.

    a. The dog woofed at the passing car.

    b. The wind whooshed through the open door.

    c. The rain pitter-pattered against the windows.

    d. The mountain lion yowled and ran away into the woods.

2. Identify the Poetic Devices

    a. Circle the instance of onomatopoeia in the poem.
    b. Assign letters to the sentences to reveal the rhyming scheme.

<u>**Rhyming Scheme (e.g. A-A-B-B)**</u>

I make a great noise	( )
Of rustling all day	( )
Like rabbit and deer	( )
Running away.	( )
But the mountains I raise	( )
Elude my embrace,	( )
Flowing over my arms	( )
And into my face.	( )

3. Write a poem of four lines, incorporating at least one instance of onomatopoeia and the enclosed rhyming scheme.

_____ (A)

_____ (B)

_____ (B)

_____ (A)

CREATE NOVEL ARTWORK (Draw something that makes a "rustling" sound.)

LESSON 36: "I HEARD A FLY BUZZ – WHEN I DIED" BY EMILY DICKINSON (ONOMATOPOEIA)

FEATURED POEM

I heard a Fly buzz - when I died –
The Stillness Round my Form
Was like the Stillness in the Air –
Between the Heaves of Storm –

The Eyes around - had wrung them dry –
And Breaths were gathering firm
For that last Onset - when the King
Be witnessed - in the Room –

I willed my Keepsakes - Signed away
What portion of me be
Assignable - and then it was
There interposed a Fly –

With Blue - uncertain - stumbling Buzz -
Between the light - and me –
And then the Windows failed - and then
I could not see to see –

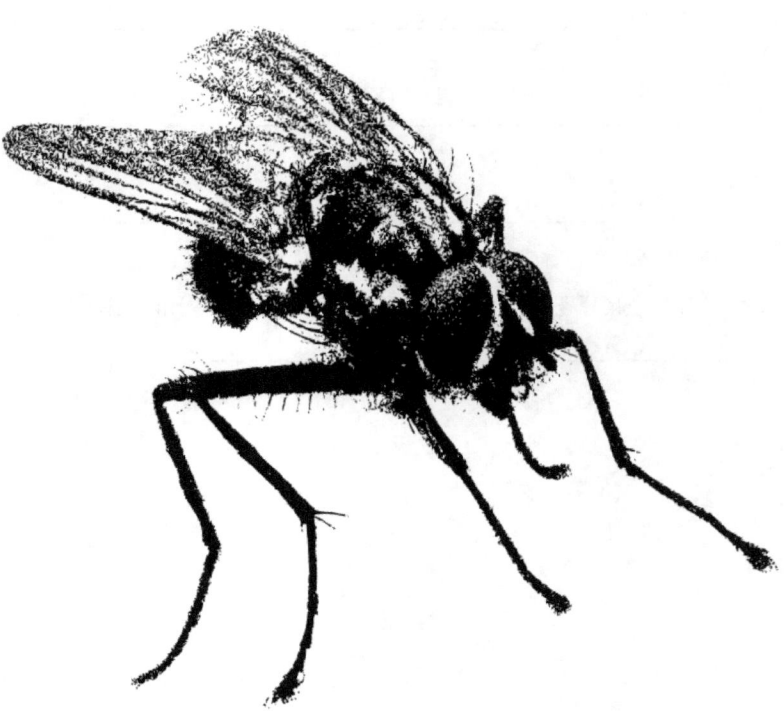

SYNOPSIS

The poem narrator reflects on the moments surrounding their death. The room is silent. The onlookers are so exhausted from their sorrow, they can no longer cry. The narrator has just signed away their worldly possessions and the King (death) is coming for them, when the fly arrives. The fly breaks the silence with its buzz and blocks the narrator's light just before she dies, plunging them into blackness. The buzz of a fly is usually unmemorable and insignificant. However, in the poem, the buzz momentously marks the instant of the narrator's death. The poem employs the onomatopoeic word "buzz" to describe the sound of the fly.

RECITE POEM, TITLE, AND POET

Practice reciting the poem, the poem title, and the name of the poet.

NARRATE THE POEM

COMPLETE COPYWORK

I heard a Fly buzz - when I died -
The Stillness Round my Form
Was like the Stillness in the Air -
Between the Heaves of Storm -

ELEMENTARY POETRY VOLUME 5: LITERARY DEVICES

COMPLETE DICTATION

_____

_____

_____

_____

DEVICE IDENTIFICATION AND EMPLOYMENT

1. Circle the onomatopoetic words in the sentences below.

    a. Something banged against the door.

    b. The booming of the bombs reverberated over the bay.

    c. The campfire popped and crackled and released a cloud of gray smoke.

    d. The soft hoot of an owl sounded in the night air.

2. Identify the Poetic Devices

    Circle the instances of onomatopoeia in the poem excerpt.

    I heard a Fly buzz - when I died -
    The Stillness Round my Form
    Was like the Stillness in the Air -
    Between the Heaves of Storm -

    The Eyes around - had wrung them dry -
    And Breaths were gathering firm
    For that last Onset - when the King
    Be witnessed - in the Room –

    With Blue - uncertain - stumbling Buzz -
    Between the light - and me -
    And then the Windows failed - and then
    I could not see to see -

3. Write a poem of six lines, incorporating at least one instance of onomatopoeia and the triplet rhyming scheme.

_____ (A)

_____ (A)

_____ (A)

_____ (B)

_____ (B)

_____ (B)

CREATE NOVEL ARTWORK (Draw something that makes a "buzzing" sound.)

LESSON ANSWERS

LESSON 1
1. "Humpty Dumpty" follows a couplet (AABB) rhyming scheme.
2. Poem rhyming scheme:
    a. ABBAABBACDDECE
    b. The start of the lesson poem follows an enclosed (ABBA) rhyming scheme.

LESSON 2
1. "Bees" follows the couplet (AABB) rhyming scheme.
2. ABCBDEFE

LESSON 3
1. "Heigh-Ho, The Carrion Crow" follows a traditional (ABAB) rhyming scheme.
2. AABCCBDDEFFE

LESSON 4
1. "How Soon Hath Time" follows an enclosed (ABBA) rhyming scheme.
2. ABABCDCDEFEF (traditional)

LESSON 5
1. Circle all instances of: Peter, Piper, picked, peck, pickled, peppers
2. Circle all instances of: Betty, Botter, bought, butter, but, bitter, batter, bit, better

LESSON 6
1. Circle the following:
    In red, all instances of: sells, seashells, seashore, so
    In blue, all instances of: she, seashells, seashore, shells, surely, sure
2.
    a. Circle every word in every line.
    b. AABBCCDD (couplet) (rhyme scheme assuming accent)

LESSON 7
1. Circle the following:
    In red, all instances of wood, would, woodchuck
    In blue, all instances of woodchuck, chuck
    In green, all instances of wood, would, woodchuck, could
2.
    a. Line 1: Circle clasps, crag, crooked
       Line 2: Circle Close, lonely, lands
       Line 5: watches, walls
    b. AAABBB
       The poem follows a triplet rhyming scheme.

LESSON 8
1. Circle the following:
    In red, all instances of Silly, Sally, swiftly, seven, south
    In blue, all instances of Shooed, sheep, shilly-shallied
2.
    a. Line 1: Circle clasps, crag, crooked
       Line 2: Circle Glory, God
       Line 3: couple, color, cow
       Line 5: Fresh, firecoal, falls, finches
       Line 6: Plotted, pierced, fold, fallow, plough
       Line 8: spare, strange
       Line 9: fickle, freckled
       Line 10: swift, slow, sweet, sour, adazzle, dim
       Line 11: fathers, forth
    b. ABCABCDBCDC

LESSON 9
1. The underlined/bolded words should be circled:
    a. The kite soared **like** a bird.
    b. Her sunburned shoulders felt as hot and dry **as** a desert.
    c. He was cold **as** ice.
    d. His face was red **like** a tomato.
    e. She was as fast **as** the wind.
2. Several examples of alliteration from the poem.
    - W: **Away** to the **window**, I **flew**
    - F: **Flew** like a **flash**
    - W: **When what** to my **wondering**
    - C: **coursers** they **came**
    - C: On, **Comet**! on, **Cupid**!
    - P: **prancing** and **pawing**
    - P: **peddler** just **opening** his **pack**
3.
    a. Similes
        i. Line 2: he - like a peddler
        ii. Line 4: cheeks – like roses; nose - like a cherry
        iii. Line 5: mouth - like a bow
        iv. Line 6: beard - white as the snow
        v. Line 8: smoke - like a wreath
        vi. Line 9-10: belly - like a bowlful of jelly
    b. AABBCCDDEE (couplet)
4. Example answers:
    a. The man was enormous as **a mammoth**.
    b. The girl sang like **an angel up in heaven**.
    c. The wolf revealed teeth as sharp as **knives**.
    d. The baby's cheeks were soft like **rose petals**.

LESSON 10

1. The underlined/bolded words should be circled:
    a. Her skin was as rough **as** sandpaper.
    b. The fabric was soft **like** a bunny.
    c. The stew was as spicy **as** a jalapeno.
    d. Her smile was as sweet **as** a lollipop.
    e. His words cut **like** a knife.

2. **You** are beautiful and faded,
    Like an old opera **tune**
    Played upon a harpsichord;
    Or **like** the sun-flooded **silks**
    Of an eighteenth-century boudoir.

3. Examples of answers include the following:
    a. The infant girl was as lovely as **a fairy princess**.
    b. The boy waved his arms like **a windmill**.
    c. The panda's belly was a round as **a beachball**.
    d. The mountains were jagged like **shattered glass**.

LESSON 11

1. The underlined/bolded words should be circled:
    a. The boy heard a crackling sound **like** a campfire.
    b. The villain was as mean **as** a junkyard dog.
    c. The plan was as diabolical **as** the devil.
    d. The bone snapped **like** a twig.
    e. She was as clever **as** a fox.

2.
    a. Simile: I wandered lonely as a cloud
    b. ABABCCDEDEFF

LESSON 12

1. The underlined/bolded words should be circled:
    a. The calm water reflected the trees **like** a mirror.
    b. He was as big **as** a giant.
    c. Her lips were as bright **as** pink rose petals.
    d. Her eyes sparkled **like** amethyst.
    e. His eyebrows looked **like** two fuzzy caterpillars.

2. Circle the following:
    a. B: When I see **birches bend** to left and right
    b. CR: As the stir **cracks** and **crazes** their enamel.
    c. T: **Toward** heaven, **till** the **tree** could bear no more,
    d. W: **One** could do **worse** than be a **swinger** of birches.

3. Similes:
    - trunks – Like girls on their hands and knees that throw their hair
    - life – like a pathless wood

LESSON 13

1. Metaphors
    a. cheeks, cherries
    b. fingers, icicles
    c. tornado, Davy
    d. blanket, night
    e. kite, bird (implied)

2. Examples of alliteration in the poem
    - TH: Why dost **thou thus**,
    - M: **Must** to thy **motions** lovers' seasons run?
    - C: Through windows, and through **curtains call** on us?
    - C/CL: I **could eclipse** and **cloud** them with a wink
    - WI: I could eclipse and cloud them **with** a **wink**

3.
    a. Metaphors from the excerpt
        - Beloved, all States (e.g. the entire world)
        - Narrator, all Princes
        - Bed, center of the universe
        - Walls, sphere surrounding the universe

        Note – additional interesting metaphors from the poem include the following:
        - Sun (implied), Saucy pedantic wretch
        - Peasants (implied), country ants
        - Blink of the narrator's eye, eclipse/clouds covering the sun

    b. ABBACDCDEE (Note: John Donne lived in 1500s-1600s, so pronunciation was a bit different!)

4. Suitable answers might include:
    a. The man was a workhorse.
    b. The girl is a whirling dervish.
    c. The wolf is a beast.
    d. The baby's toes were rosy little piggies.

LESSON 14

1. Metaphors
    a. curator, dinosaur
    b. Sally, cat
    c. bedroom, disaster zone
    d. teeth (implied), daggers
    e. garden, paradise

2.
    a. Metaphors:
        - sun (implied) – eye of heaven
        - beauty/youth of beloved (implied) - eternal summer
        - death of beloved - death's shade
        - poem – eternal lines to Time
    b. ABABCDCD

LESSON 15

1. Metaphors
    a. old man (implied), firecracker
    b. ballroom, fairyland
    c. sun (implied), oven
    d. truck, monster
    e. child, dervish
2.
    a. Metaphors:
        - narrator's thoughts, grain
        - sky (implied), night's face
        - narrator's beloved (implied), fair creature of an hour
    b. ABABCDCD (traditional)

LESSON 16

1. Metaphors
    a. fingernails, scissors
    b. nose, mountain
    c. backyard, jungle
    d. girl, princess
    e. nose, faucet

2. Examples of alliteration in the poem
    - S: When the wind **stirs soft** through the **springing grass**,
    - S: And the river **flows** like a **stream** of **glass**;
    - B: When his wing is **bruised** and his **bosom** sore,—
    - B: When he **beats** his **bars** and he would be free;

3. Simile: And the river flows **like** a stream of glass; (compares river, stream of glass)

4.
    a. Metaphors:
        - oppressed people (implied), bird
        - oppression (implied), cage
    b. ABAABAA

LESSON 17

1. Personified objects:
    a. leaf
    b. sun
    c. mower
    d. pie
    e. siren

2. Examples of alliteration in the poem
    - W: To **watch** his **woods** fill up with **snow**.
    - S: The only other **sound's** the **sweep**
    - D: The **woods** are lovely, **dark** and **deep**,

3.
    a. Personification: horse personified as "thinking it queer" and "asking if there is some mistake"
    b. AABACCDC

4. Example suitable answers:
    a. The dog winked before jumping up on the dining room table and stealing the roast chicken.
    b. The ticking clock scolded us that the deadline was approaching.
    c. The wolf howled, mournfully lamenting the onset of winter.
    d. The tired house groaned as we stepped inside.

LESSON 18

1. Personified objects:
    a. ocean
    b. fire
    c. bird
    d. earth
    e. welt

2. Circle terms and phrases that personify the setting sun such as:
    - sweeping/brooms
    - housewife
    - dusting
    - dropping raveling/thread
    - aprons fly

LESSON 19

1. Personified objects:
    a. leaf
    b. daisy
    c. snake
    d. ring
    e. roof

2.
    a. Circle whispering/whispered terms that personify the scythe.
    b. ABCABDECDGEHGH

LESSON 20

1. Personified objects:
    a. cockroach
    b. star
    c. pencil
    d. big dog
    e. llama

2. Examples of similes in the poem:
    - And neigh **like** Boanerges; (compares train, Boanerges*)

    Note: *Boanerges* refers to a loud public speaker or the "sons of thunder" from the Christian Bible.

    - Then, punctual **as** a star, (compares train, star)

3. Circle terms and phrases that personify the train such as:
    - lap the miles
    - lick the valleys
    - feed itself
    - step around
    - supercilious
    - peer
    - pare
    - crawl
    - complaining
    - hooting
    - chase itself

LESSON 21

1. Example projections of foreshadowed events:
    a. Timmy will fall behind, placing the pack of children in peril as they go back to rescue him.
    b. Sally will become injured, but Mark will be unable to carry her to safety.
    c. Peter will need to call his mother but will be unable to as he's forgotten his phone.
    d. The woman inside the house kidnaps the boy, holding his prisoner.
    e. Larry will meet his Uncle Jim, who will earn Larry's trust and later steal all of Larry's money.
2. A few examples of alliteration from the poem:
    - R: In a **rush** of **rain**.
    - D: I remembered a **darkened doorway**
    - S: Where we **stood** while the **storm swept** by,
    - R: For the street was a **river** of **rain**,
    - L: In the **lamp light's** stain.
3.
    a. Circle terms and phrases that foreshadow future events:
        - Wild spring rain and thunder – foreshadows a tumultuous future for the paramours
        - Your eyes said more…than your lips would ever say – the paramours may be separated and not speak in the future (alternatively, it could just be an infinitely profound look no amount of words could match.)
    b. ABCB
4. Examples of foreshadowing:
    a. If only I had known that she was allergic to bee stings, disaster may have been averted.
    b. "Jimmy, be sure to remember to put the dog out," said my mother.
    c. A crystal ball might have told me not to get in that car and changed my future.
    d. "Don't forget your inhaler," my teacher warned.

LESSON 22

1. Potential predictions:
    a. The house will collapse.
    b. The man will suffer a heart problem.
    c. Larry will hurt his head, due to a lack of helmet.
    d. The woman in black is a ghost.
    e. The ringing bell is warning the town that the dam is about to break, flooding the town.
2. A few examples of alliteration from the poem:
    - B: When Spring **brings back blue** days and fair.
    - S: On **some scarred slope** of battered hill,
    - S: Pillowed in silk and scented down,
3.
    a. Circle the entire excerpt – which foreshadows the death, the place of death, and the timing of death.
    b. AABCBCDD
4. Examples of foreshadowing:
    a. Little did I know at the time, **but she would one day become my wife**.
    b. My future might have been very different if I hadn't **missed that train**.
    c. "If you let me borrow **your phone**, I promise I won't break it," my sister said.
    d. If I had just remembered to **lock the front door**, things would have turned out differently.

LESSON 23

1. Potential predictions:
    a. Something spooky will happen.
    b. Someone who has a crush on Suzy will later be revealed.
    c. Part of the town is being evacuated due to a gas leak.
    d. Spooky special effects will scare the protagonist.
    e. The protagonist will later save a school bus full of children and its driver.
2. A few examples of alliteration from the poem:
    - F: In **form** and **feature**, **face** and limb,
    - K: It puzzled all our **kith** and **kin**,
    - W: As **we were** being **washed** by nurse,
    - B: And **buried brother** John.
3.
    a. Examples of foreshadowing that the twin mix-ups would have negative effects:
        o Folks got taking me for him
        o It reached a fearful pitch
    b. ABACDCD

LESSON 24

1. Potential predictions:
    a. Barry's father will recover from his illness.
    b. The valedictorian will have good luck in her future.
    c. David will earn a perfect score on his spelling test.
    d. Poor Annie is rushed to the hospital by ambulance.
2. A few examples of alliteration from the poem:
    - G: Did **gyre** and **gimble** in the wabe;
    - C: The jaws that bite, the **claws** that **catch**!
    - SN: The vorpal blade went **snicker**-**snack**!
    - B: Come to my arms, my **beamish boy**!
3.
    a. Examples of foreshadowing:
        o Beware the Jabberwock, my son
        o Beware the Jubjub bird and…Bandersnatch!
    b. ABAB (traditional)

LESSON 25

1. Allusions:
    a. Alludes to the Biblical Noah's Ark.
    b. Alludes to Arthurian Legend.
    c. Alludes to Cupid, Roman god of romantic love and desire.
    d. Alludes to Leonardo da Vinci's famous portrait, Mona Lisa.
2. A few examples of alliteration from the poem:
    - S: **Some say** the world will end in fire,
    - S: **Some say** in **ice**.
    - F: I hold with those who **favor fire**.
3.
    a. Circle "the world will end in fire."
    b. ABAABCBCB
4. Examples of suitable answers:
    a. Sarah felt like Alice in Wonderland when she **saw a rabbit run by her**.
    b. I imagined his Pinocchio nose growing when he **told a lie**.
    c. The girl **wore a blue dress and had a little dog** just like Dorothy in the Wizard of Oz.
    d. Like the Star of Bethlehem, **one star blazed brighter than the others in the night sky**.

LESSON 26

1. Allusions:
    a. Alludes to the Garden of Eden in the Christian Bible.
    b. Alludes to Icarus in Greek mythology, who ignored his father's warnings and flew to close to the sun. Icarus' wax wings melted, and he plummeted to his death.
    c. Alludes to the Cheshire Cat in Alice in Wonderland.
    d. Alludes to Superman's one weakness of Kryptonite.
2. A few examples of alliteration from the poem:
    - W: Getting and spending, **we** lay **waste** our **powers**;—
    - B: This Sea that **bares** her **bosom** to the moon;
    - G: It moves us not. **Great God**! I'd rather be
3. Simile example: The winds… are up-gathered now **like** sleeping flowers. (winds, flowers)
4. Personified objects:
    - The poem personifies the sea as a woman that "bares her bosom to the moon."
    - The poem personifies the winds as a howling creature.
5.
    a. Circle "Proteus" and "Triton," allusions from Greek mythology.
    b. ABABAB (traditional)
6. Examples of suitable answers:
    a. When I **pulled a rabbit out of a hat,** the little boy stared at me and said, "You're a wizard! Just like Merlin!"
    b. The boy looked worried because **his brother was late**, so I tossed him my phone and said, "Why don't you phone home, like the alien?"
    c. Just like Cinderella, she **ran down a flight of stairs and lost her shoe**.
    d. I called the little girl Tarzan because **she loved the swings best of all at the playground**.

LESSON 27

1. Allusions:
    a. Alludes to King Midas from Greek mythology. Everything King Midas touches turns into gold.
    b. Alludes to the Wizard of Oz.
    c. Alludes to the Christian Bible.
    d. Alludes to the Greek mythological hero, Achilles, whose only vulnerability was his heel.
2. Alliteration examples:
    - H: Another name our **hearts hath** stirred,
    - M: Is **music** and **melody**:
3. Metaphor examples:
    - Lily of lilies He (Jesus Christ, lily)
    - Rose of roses, soon to be (Jesus Christ, rose)
    - And Jesus Christ...Is the Lamb of God: (Jesus Christ, lamb)
4.
    a. Circle "Jesus Christ our Lord" and "Crowned with thorns," allusions the Christian Bible.
    b. ABACCCC

LESSON 28

1. Allusions:
    a. Alludes to King Arthur's Mantle of Invisibility from Arthurian Legend.
    b. Alludes to Vincent van Gogh's painting "The Starry Night."
    c. Alludes to the box Pandora opened in Greek mythology.
    d. Alludes to the Biblical story of the boy David triumphing over the giant Goliath.
2. Simile examples:
    - The gemmy bridle glitter'd free, **Like** to some branch of stars we see (bridle, stars)
    - The helmet and the helmet-feather Burn'd **like** one burning flame together, (burning helmet and feather, one flame)
    - **Like** some bold seër in a trance, (Lady of Shalott, seer)
3. Foreshadowing examples:
    - As Camelot is associated with Sir Lancelot and is the ultimate destination of her body on the river, this passage foretells the Lady of Shalott's downfall and its association with Camelot.
      A curse is on her if she stay
      To look down to Camelot.
      She knows not what the curse may be,
      And so she weaveth steadily,
    - There exists an old superstition that breaking a mirror leads to bad luck. The mirror cracking in the poem foreshadows the Lady of Shalott's misfortune.
4.
    a. Circle the following Allusions to Arthurian Legend:
        - knights at Camelot
        - Lancelot
        - Lady of Shalott
    b. AAAABAAAB

LESSON 29

1. Hyperbole Explanations:
    a. The person may be taking a long time, but they aren't really taking forever.
    b. No one walked 50 miles to school every day. It would take too long (around 20 hours). Plus, it is impossible for it to be uphill both ways.
    c. It's almost certain the child will speak again to their mother.
    d. Jokes might make you laugh and lose your breath, but they won't kill you.
2. A few examples of alliteration from the poem:
    - S: The foe long since in **silence slept**;
    - S: Alike the conqueror **silent sleeps**;
    - S: Down the dark **stream** which **seaward creeps**.
3.
    a. Circle the "shot heard round the world."
    b. ABABCDCD (traditional)
4. Example answers:
    a. She turned cartwheels as fast as **a pinwheel spinning in a stiff breeze**.
    b. He grew as tall as a **pine tree**.
    c. I'm so hungry I could eat a **dish filled with one hundred scoops of ice cream**.
    d. She ran so fast **she outran the sunbeams**.
    e. I'm so tired, I could **sleep for eons**.

LESSON 30

1. Hyperbole Explanations:
    a. It is physically impossible for a human to eat a million pancakes at once.
    b. It is physically impossible for a human to eat an entire cow at once.
    c. Perhaps one day humans will travel to Jupiter, but that time is likely far off and will not occur in our lifetimes.
2. Two examples of similes from the poem:
    - O my Love is **like** a red, red rose (Narrator's love for his lass, rose)
    - O my Love is **like** the melody (Narrator's love for his lass, melody)
3.
    a. Circle the following examples of hyperbole:
        - love thee…Till a' the seas gang dry
        - Till…the rocks melt wi' the sun
    b. ABABCDCD (traditional)
4. Example answers:
    a. I ate as much as **a Titan**.
    b. He walked so slow **a snail could have easily passed him**.
    c. The ice skater spun faster **than a jet turbine**.
    d. The bag was as heavy as a **tow truck**.
    e. It snowed so much**, the snow piles could have covered skyscrapers**.

LESSON 31

1. Hyperbole Explanations:
    a. Love doesn't generate physical light.
    b. A ton of typical material would not fit inside a backpack.
    c. No humans are as tall as mountains.
    d. It unlikely "she" scurries at the sight of humans and hides in hole all day long.
2. A few examples of alliteration from the poem:
    - ON/W: For they thought if only Casey could get **one whack**, at that
    - S: And so, on that stricken multitude a death-like **silence sat**,
    - AU/AW: But the scornful look from Casey, and the **audience** was **awed**;
3. Two examples of similes from the poem:
    - And so, on that stricken multitude a death-**like** silence sat, (death, silence)
    - …there went up a muffled roar, Like the beating of the storm-waves (roar of crowd, storm-waves)
4.
    a. Circle the following examples of hyperbole:
        o it's likely they'd have killed him had not Casey raised his hand
        o the air is shattered
    b. AABBCCDD (couplet)

LESSON 32

1. Hyperbole Explanations:
    a. Polar bears live in temperatures well below zero in the winter. If it was this cold inside the house, the pipes would burst.
    b. If you didn't have a drop of blood left, you'd be dead.
    c. Human lifespans don't last anywhere near 1000 years, so humans cannot sleep that long.
2. Examples of alliteration from the poem:
    - K/QU: In **keen** and **quivering** ratio
    - P: **Sharp pittances** of years –
3.
    a. Circle "coffers heaped with tears!"
    b. ABCBDEFE

LESSON 33

1. Circle the following onomatopoetic words:
    a. thud
    b. buzzed
    c. meowed
    d. smacked
2. A few examples of alliteration:
    - M: What a world of **merriment** their **melody** foretells!
    - R: In a sort of **Runic rhyme**,
    - B: **Brazen bells**!
    - T: What **tale** of **terror**, now, their **turbulency tells**!
    - M: At the **melancholy menace** of their tone!
3. A few instances of personification: turtledove gloating, bells screaming, bells being horrified, bells shrieking, and bells groaning from their throats.

4.
- a. Circle the following:
  - o tinkle, tinkle, tinkle
  - o tintinabulation
  - o jingling
  - o tinkling
- b. ABBBCDCCDEEBB

LESSON 34

1. Circle the following onomatopoetic words:
   a. chugged
   b. whizzed, exploded, pop
   c. cracked
   d. sizzled
2.
   - a. Circle the following:
     - o tap
     - o scratch
     - o spurt
   - b. ABCCBADEFFED

LESSON 35

1. Circle the following onomatopoetic words:
   a. woofed
   b. whooshed
   c. pitter-pattered
   d. yowled
2.
   - a. Circle the following: rustling
   - b. ABCBDEFE

LESSON 36

1. Circle the following onomatopoetic words:
   a. banged
   b. booming, reverberated
   c. popped, crackled
   d. hoot
2. Circle the following: the two instances of "buzz"

REFERENCES AND ADDITIONAL READING

1. ***Cover Image***
   a. Title: "Take the Fair Face of Woman, and Gently Suspending, With Butterflies, Flowers, and Jewels Attending, Thus Your Fairy is Made of Most Beautiful Things"
   b. Artist: Sophie Gengembre Anderson
   c. Original Source: commons.wikimedia.org/wiki/File:SophieAndersonTakethefairfaceofWoman.jpg
   d. License: The author died in 1903, so this work is in the public domain in its country of origin and other countries and areas where the copyright term is the author's life plus 100 years or less. This work is in the public domain in the United States because it was published (or registered with the U.S. Copyright Office) before January 1, 1925.

2. ***Lesson 1 Poem - Remember***
   a. Rossetti, Christina Georgina, 1830-1894, Dante Gabriel Rossetti, Bradbury & Evans, and Macmillan & Co. Goblin Market And Other Poems. Cambridge: Macmillan and Co., 1862..
   b. License: The author died in 1894, so this work is in the public domain in its country of origin and other countries and areas where the copyright term is the author's life plus 100 years or less. This work is in the public domain in the United States because it was published (or registered with the U.S. Copyright Office) before January 1, 1925.

3. ***Lesson 2 Poem – All Things Bright and Beautiful***
   a. Alexander, Cecil Frances, 1818-1895. Hymns for Little Children. 66th ed. London: Masters, 1887 [1848.].
   b. License: The author died in 1895, so this work is in the public domain in its country of origin and other countries and areas where the copyright term is the author's life plus 100 years or less. This work is in the public domain in the United States because it was published (or registered with the U.S. Copyright Office) before January 1, 1925.

4. ***Lesson 3 Poem – Christmas Carol***
   a. Dunbar, Paul Laurence, 1872-1906. The Complete Poems of Paul Laurence Dunbar. New York: Dodd, Mead, and Company, 1913.
   b. License: The author died in 1906, so this work is in the public domain in its country of origin and other countries and areas where the copyright term is the author's life plus 100 years or less. This work is in the public domain in the United States because it was published (or registered with the U.S. Copyright Office) before January 1, 1925.

5. ***Lesson 4 Poem – Merry Autumn***
   a. Dunbar, Paul Laurence, 1872-1906. The Complete Poems of Paul Laurence Dunbar. New York: Dodd, Mead, and Company, 1913.
   b. License: The author died in 1906, so this work is in the public domain in its country of origin and other countries and areas where the copyright term is the author's life plus 100 years or less. This work is in the public domain in the United States because it was published (or registered with the U.S. Copyright Office) before January 1, 1925.

6. ***Lesson 5 Poem – The Butter Betty Bought***
   a. Wells, Carolyn, 1862-1942, and Oliver Herford. The Jingle Book. New York: Macmillan, 1899.
   b. License: This work is in the public domain in the United States because it was published (or registered with the U.S. Copyright Office) before January 1, 1925.

7. ***Lesson 6 Illustration***
   a. "Siege of Belgrade" (Nándorfehérvár) (1588, {PD-US})
   b. Source: https://commons.wikimedia.org/wiki/File:Siege_of_Belgrade_(N%C3%A1ndorfeh%C3%A9rv%C3%A1r)_1456.jpg
   c. License: This work is in the public domain in its country of origin and other countries and areas where the copyright term is the author's life plus 100 years or fewer. This work is in the public domain in the

United States because it was published (or registered with the U.S. Copyright Office) before January 1, 1925.

8. ***Lesson 6 Poem – The Siege of Belgrade***
   a. Alaric Alexander Watts (Bliss, Carman, Editor), 1797–1864. The World's Best Poetry. Philadelphia: John D. Morris & Co., 1904.
   b. License: The author died in 1864, so this work is in the public domain in its country of origin and other countries and areas where the copyright term is the author's life plus 100 years or less. This work is in the public domain in the United States because it was published (or registered with the U.S. Copyright Office) before January 1, 1925.

9. ***Lesson 7 Poem – The Eagle***
   a. Tennyson, Lord Alfred (Emerson Ralph Waldo, Editor), 1809-1892. Parnassus: An Anthology of Poetry. Boston: Houghton, Osgood and Company, 1880.
   b. License: The author died in 1892, so this work is in the public domain in its country of origin and other countries and areas where the copyright term is the author's life plus 100 years or less. This work is in the public domain in the United States because it was published (or registered with the U.S. Copyright Office) before January 1, 1925.

10. ***Lesson 8 Poem – Pied Beauty***
    a. Hopkins, Gerard Manley, 1844-1889. Poems of Gerard Manley Hopkins. London: Milford, 1918.
    b. License: The author died in 1889, so this work is in the public domain in its country of origin and other countries and areas where the copyright term is the author's life plus 100 years or less. This work is in the public domain in the United States because it was published (or registered with the U.S. Copyright Office) before January 1, 1925.

11. ***Lesson 9 Illustrations***
    a. "Twas the Night Before Christmas: A Visit from St. Nicholas" by Clement Moore. Illustrations by Jessie Willcox Smith. (1912, {PD-US})
    b. Source: https://www.gutenberg.org/files/17135/17135-h/17135-h.htm
    c. License: This work is in the public domain in the United States because it was published (or registered with the U.S. Copyright Office) before January 1, 1925.

12. ***Lesson 9 Poem – A Visit from St. Nicholas***
    a. Moore, Clement Clarke, 1779-1863. Troy, *New York Sentinel* on 23 December 1823.
    b. License: The author died in 1863, so this work is in the public domain in its country of origin and other countries and areas where the copyright term is the author's life plus 100 years or less. This work is in the public domain in the United States because it was published (or registered with the U.S. Copyright Office) before January 1, 1925.

13. ***Lesson 10 Poem – A Lady***
    a. Lowell, Amy (Rittenhouse, Jessie B., editor), 1874-1925. The Second Book of Modern Verse. Boston: Houghton Mifflin Company, 1920.
    b. License: The author died in 1925, so this work is in the public domain in its country of origin and other countries and areas where the copyright term is the author's life plus 95 years or less. This work is in the public domain in the United States because it was published (or registered with the U.S. Copyright Office) before January 1, 1925.

14. ***Lesson 11 Poem – I Wandered Lonely as a Cloud***
    a. Wordsworth, William (Braithwaite, William Stanley, editor), 1770–1850. The Book of Georgian Verse. New York: Brentano's, 1909.
    b. License: The author died in 1850, so this work is in the public domain in its country of origin and other countries and areas where the copyright term is the author's life plus 100 years or less. This work is in the public domain in the United States because it was published (or registered with the U.S. Copyright Office) before January 1, 1925.

15. ***Lesson 12 Poem – Birches***
    a. Frost, Robert (Untermeyer, Louis, editor), 1864-1963. Modern American Poetry. New York: Harcourt, Brace and Howe, 1919.

16. ***Lesson 13 Poem – The Sun Rising***
    a. Donne, John, 1572–1631. The Poems of John Donne. London: Lawrence & Bullen, 1896.
    b. License: The author died in 1631, so this work is in the public domain in its country of origin and other countries and areas where the copyright term is the author's life plus 100 years or less. This work is in the public domain in the United States because it was published (or registered with the U.S. Copyright Office) before January 1, 1925.
17. ***Lesson 14 Poem – Shall I Compare Thee?***
    a. Shakespeare, William (Carman, Bliss, editor), 1564–1616. The World's Best Poetry. Philadelphia: John D. Morris & Co., 1904.
    b. License: The author died in 1616, so this work is in the public domain in its country of origin and other countries and areas where the copyright term is the author's life plus 100 years or less. This work is in the public domain in the United States because it was published (or registered with the U.S. Copyright Office) before January 1, 1925.
18. ***Lesson 15 Poem – When I Have Fears***
    a. Keats, John (Quiller-Couch, Arthur, editor), 1795–1821. The Oxford Book of English Verse: 1250–1900. Oxford: Clarendon, 1919, [c1901].
    b. License: The author died in 1821, so this work is in the public domain in its country of origin and other countries and areas where the copyright term is the author's life plus 100 years or less. This work is in the public domain in the United States because it was published (or registered with the U.S. Copyright Office) before January 1, 1925.
19. ***Lesson 15 Illustration – When I Have Fears***
    a. "Caged Bird in a Tree" by Alfred Batty. (1872, {PD-US})
    b. Source: https://commons.wikimedia.org/wiki/File:Caged_Bird_in_Tree.jpg
    c. License: This work is in the public domain in the United States because it was published (or registered with the U.S. Copyright Office) before January 1, 1925.
20. ***Lesson 16 Poem – Sympathy***
    a. Dunbar, Paul Laurence, 1872-1906. The Complete Poems of Paul Laurence Dunbar. New York: Dodd, Mead, and Company, 1913.
    b. License: The author died in 1906, so this work is in the public domain in its country of origin and other countries and areas where the copyright term is the author's life plus 100 years or less. This work is in the public domain in the United States because it was published (or registered with the U.S. Copyright Office) before January 1, 1925.
21. ***Lesson 17 Poem – Stopping by the Woods on a Snowing Evening***
    a. Frost, Robert, 1874-1963. New Hampshire, Henry Holt and Company, 1923.
    b. License: This work is in the public domain in the United States because it was published (or registered with the U.S. Copyright Office) before January 1, 1925.
22. ***Lesson 18 Poem – She Sweeps with Many-Colored Brooms***
    a. Dickinson, Emily, 1830-1886. The Complete Poems of Emily Dickinson. Boston: Little, Brown, and Company, 1924.
    b. License: The author died in 1886, so this work is in the public domain in its country of origin and other countries and areas where the copyright term is the author's life plus 100 years or less. This work is in the public domain in the United States because it was published (or registered with the U.S. Copyright Office) before January 1, 1925.
23. ***Lesson 19 Poem – Mowing***
    a. Frost, Robert, 1874-1963. A Boy's Will, New York: Henry Holt and Company, 1915.
    b. License: This work is in the public domain in the United States because it was published (or registered with the U.S. Copyright Office) before January 1, 1925.

24. ***Lesson 20 Poem – The Railway Train***
    a. Dickinson, Emily, 1830-1886. <u>The Complete Poems of Emily Dickinson</u>. Boston: Little, Brown, and Company, 1924.
    b. License: The author died in 1886, so this work is in the public domain in its country of origin and other countries and areas where the copyright term is the author's life plus 100 years or less. This work is in the public domain in the United States because it was published (or registered with the U.S. Copyright Office) before January 1, 1925.
25. ***Lesson 21 Poem – Spring Rain***
    a. Teasdale, Sara, 1884-1933. <u>Love Songs</u>. The Macmillan Company, 1917.
    b. License: The author died in 1933, so this work is in the public domain in its country of origin and other countries and areas where the copyright term is the author's life plus 85 years or less. This work is in the public domain in the United States because it was published (or registered with the U.S. Copyright Office) before January 1, 1925.
26. ***Lesson 22 Poem – I Have a Rendezvous with Death***
    a. Seeger, Alan, 1888–1916. <u>Modern American Poetry</u>. New York: Harcourt, Brace and Howe, 1919.
    b. License: The author died in 1916, so this work is in the public domain in its country of origin and other countries and areas where the copyright term is the author's life plus 100 years or less. This work is in the public domain in the United States because it was published (or registered with the U.S. Copyright Office) before January 1, 1925.
27. ***Lesson 23 Poem – The Twins***
    a. Leigh, Henry Sambrooke, 1837–1883. <u>Carols of Cockayne</u>. 3th ed. Chatto and Windus, 1874.
    b. License: The author died in 1883, so this work is in the public domain in its country of origin and other countries and areas where the copyright term is the author's life plus 100 years or less. This work is in the public domain in the United States because it was published (or registered with the U.S. Copyright Office) before January 1, 1925.
28. ***Lesson 24 Poem – Jabberwocky***
    a. Carroll, Lewis, 1832–1898. <u>A Victorian Anthology, 1837–1895</u>. Cambridge: Riverside Press, 1895.
    b. License: The author died in 1898, so this work is in the public domain in its country of origin and other countries and areas where the copyright term is the author's life plus 100 years or less. This work is in the public domain in the United States because it was published (or registered with the U.S. Copyright Office) before January 1, 1925.
29. ***Lesson 25 Poem – Fire and Ice***
    a. Frost, Robert, 1874-1963. *Harper's Magazine*, December 1920.
    b. License: This work is in the public domain in the United States because it was published (or registered with the U.S. Copyright Office) before January 1, 1925.
30. ***Lesson 26 Poem – The World Is Too Much with Us***
    a. Wordsworth, William (Palgrave, Francis T., editor), 1770–1850. <u>The Golden Treasury</u>. London: Macmillan, 1875.
    b. License: The author died in 1850, so this work is in the public domain in its country of origin and other countries and areas where the copyright term is the author's life plus 100 years or less. This work is in the public domain in the United States because it was published (or registered with the U.S. Copyright Office) before January 1, 1925.
31. ***Lesson 26 Illustration***
    a. "Proteus-Alciato" by Jörg Breu the Elder, displayed in the Book of Emblems by Andrea Alciato. (1475, {PD-US})
    b. Source: https://en.wikipedia.org/wiki/File:Proteus-Alciato.gif
    c. License: This work is in the public domain in the United States because it was published (or registered with the U.S. Copyright Office) before January 1, 1925.
32. ***Lesson 27 Poem – Christmas Day***
    a. Rossetti, Christina Georgina, 1830-1894, <u>Verses</u>. E. & J. B. Young, 1893..

b. License: The author died in 1894, so this work is in the public domain in its country of origin and other countries and areas where the copyright term is the author's life plus 100 years or less. This work is in the public domain in the United States because it was published (or registered with the U.S. Copyright Office) before January 1, 1925.

33. ***Lesson 28 Poem – The Lady of Shalott***
    a. Tennyson, Lord Alfred (Quiller-Couch, Arthur, editor), 1809–1892. <u>The Oxford Book of English Verse: 1250–1900</u>, Oxford: Clarendon, 1919, [c1901].
    b. License: The author died in 1892, so this work is in the public domain in its country of origin and other countries and areas where the copyright term is the author's life plus 100 years or less. This work is in the public domain in the United States because it was published (or registered with the U.S. Copyright Office) before January 1, 1925.

34. ***Lesson 29 Poem – Concord Hymn***
    a. Emerson, Ralph Waldo, 1803–1882. <u>Yale Book of American Verse</u>. New Haven: Yale University Press, 1912.
    b. License: The author died in 1882, so this work is in the public domain in its country of origin and other countries and areas where the copyright term is the author's life plus 100 years or less. This work is in the public domain in the United States because it was published (or registered with the U.S. Copyright Office) before January 1, 1925.

35. ***Lesson 30 Poem – A Red, Red, Rose***
    a. Burns, Robert, 1759–1796. <u>The Oxford Book of English Verse: 1250–1900</u>. Oxford: Clarendon, 1919, [c1901].
    b. License: The author died in 1796, so this work is in the public domain in its country of origin and other countries and areas where the copyright term is the author's life plus 100 years or less. This work is in the public domain in the United States because it was published (or registered with the U.S. Copyright Office) before January 1, 1925.

36. ***Lesson 31 Poem – Casey at the Bat***
    a. Thayer, Ernest Lawrence, 1863–1940. <u>The World's Wit and Humor: An Encyclopedia in 15 Volumes</u>. New York: The Review of Reviews Company, 1906.
    b. License: The author died in 1940, so this work is in the public domain in its country of origin and other countries and areas where the copyright term is the author's life plus 80 years or less. This work is in the public domain in the United States because it was published (or registered with the U.S. Copyright Office) before January 1, 1925.

37. ***Lesson 32 Poem – For Each Ecstatic Instant***
    a. Dickinson, Emily, 1830-1886. <u>The Complete Poems of Emily Dickinson</u>. Boston: Little, Brown, and Company, 1924.
    b. License: The author died in 1886, so this work is in the public domain in its country of origin and other countries and areas where the copyright term is the author's life plus 100 years or less. This work is in the public domain in the United States because it was published (or registered with the U.S. Copyright Office) before January 1, 1925.

38. ***Lesson 33 Poem – The Bells***
    a. Poe, Edgar Allen, 1809–1849. <u>Yale Book of American Verse</u>. New Haven: Yale University Press, 1912.
    b. License: The author died in 1849, so this work is in the public domain in its country of origin and other countries and areas where the copyright term is the author's life plus 100 years or less. This work is in the public domain in the United States because it was published (or registered with the U.S. Copyright Office) before January 1, 1925.

39. ***Lesson 34 Poem – Meeting at Night***
    a. Browning, Robert (Reynolds, Myra, Editor), 1812-1889. <u>Selections from the Poems and Plays of Robert Browning</u>. Scott, Foresman, and Company, 1909.
    b. License: The author died in 1889, so this work is in the public domain in its country of origin and other countries and areas where the copyright term is the author's life plus 100 years or less. This work is in

the public domain in the United States because it was published (or registered with the U.S. Copyright Office) before January 1, 1925.

40. ***Lesson 35 Poem – Gathering Leaves***
    a. Frost, Robert, 1874-1963. New Hampshire, Henry Holt and Company, 1923.
    b. License: This work is in the public domain in the United States because it was published (or registered with the U.S. Copyright Office) before January 1, 1925.
41. ***Lesson 36 Poem – I heard a fly buzz – when I died***
    a. Dickinson, Emily, 1830-1886. The Complete Poems of Emily Dickinson. Boston: Little, Brown, and Company, 1924.
    b. License: The author died in 1886, so this work is in the public domain in its country of origin and other countries and areas where the copyright term is the author's life plus 100 years or less. This work is in the public domain in the United States because it was published (or registered with the U.S. Copyright Office) before January 1, 1925.
42. ***All Other Clipart and Images. Open Clipart. openclipart.org. n.p. ({PD-US})***
43. ***All Definitions. Wiktionary: Public Domain Sources. en.wiktionary.org. n.p. ({PD-US}).***

ABOUT THE AUTHOR

Sonja Glumich is a scientist, educator, wife, and mother who is inspired by Charlotte Mason's living works approach to homeschooling. She is the founder of Under the Home (underthehome.org), an online homeschool curriculum featuring free courses in art history, poetry, prose, music, history, science, studio art, mathematics, reading, and Shakespeare. Sonja's husband, Chris, homeschools their three school-aged children using the Under the Home curriculum as featured in this book.

Sonja graduated magna cum laude with bachelor's degrees in biology, chemistry, and computer science and later earned a master's degree in information technology. She has also completed education classes and student teaching leading to certification to teach secondary science.

Sonja has experience teaching students of all ages, from preschool to graduate school, including as a middle school and high school science public school teacher. She has also served as an Adjunct Professor for Syracuse University and co-created two graduate-level cyber courses. She currently works as a computer scientist for the Air Force Research Laboratory. Her current research and education interests are security systems engineering, cyber vulnerability assessments, and everything homeschooling.

www.ingramcontent.com/pod-product-compliance
Lightning Source LLC
LaVergne TN
LVHW081357060426
835510LV00016B/1872